In a world filled with countless voices and distractions vying for our attention, it can be increasingly difficult to establish a consistent and meaningful rhythm in our time with the Lord. *Seven Minutes with Jesus for Men* offers a clear and transformative path, guiding you through a sixty-day journey that reveals Jesus in a fresh and personal way.

This book invites us to encounter King Jesus daily and experience the profound difference He makes in our lives. Ray Cummings is a dedicated student of God's Word and, more importantly, a true friend of Jesus. His deep knowledge and genuine faith give him the authority and the heart to lead us into a deeper relationship with our Savior.

The best part? It all begins with just seven minutes with the Father—yet the impact will echo into eternity.

—*Luiz F. Cardoso*
Regional Director, UK and Ireland, M4 Europe
Senior Pastor, Glasgow Story Church, Glasgow, Scotland

Dr. Ray Cummings has gifted the body of Christ with *Seven Minutes with Jesus for Men*. In this devotional journey through the Gospel of John, he masterfully brings timeless truth into the rhythms of daily life, making the profound simplicity of the gospel accessible, applicable, and deeply enriching. Each daily reflection is rich in biblical insight and practical wisdom, inviting readers to understand and experience Christ's transforming power. If you desire a deeper faith, a closer walk with Jesus, and a greater appreciation for the gospel's relevance to your everyday life, this book is for you. I highly recommend it!

—*Dr. Scott Hanberry*
Executive Director, Homes of Hope for Children

I encourage every man to spend seven minutes daily with Jesus studying and meditating on this excellent devotional book. Dr. Ray Cummings presents this work to every man who desires to grow spiritually and walk closer to the Lord.
—*Roberto Sequeira*
Missionary and National Field Partner
Baptist Medical and Dental Mission International,
Managua, Nicaragua

SEVEN MINUTES
— with —
JESUS
for Men
Applying the Gospel of John to Everyday Life

A 60-Day Devotional
RAY CUMMINGS

Unless otherwise noted, Scripture quotations are from the *Holy Bible, New Living Translation*, copyright © 1996, 2004, 2015 by Tyndale House Foundation. Used by permission of Tyndale House Publishers, Carol Stream, Illinois 60188. All rights reserved. Scripture quotations marked (NIV) are taken from the *Holy Bible, New International Version*®, *NIV*®. Copyright © 1973, 1978, 1984, 2011 by Biblica, Inc.™ Used by permission of Zondervan. All rights reserved worldwide. www.zondervan.com. The "NIV" and "New International Version" are trademarks registered in the United States Patent and Trademark Office by Biblica, Inc.® Scripture quotations marked (NKJV) are taken from the *New King James Version*.® Copyright © 1982 by Thomas Nelson, Inc. Used by permission. All rights reserved. Scripture quotations marked (MSG) are taken from *The Message: The Bible in Contemporary Language* by Eugene H. Peterson, © 1993, 1994, 1995, 1996, 2000, 2001, 2002. Used by permission of NavPress Publishing Group. All rights reserved. Represented by Tyndale House Publishers, Inc. Scripture quotations marked (KJV) are taken from the King James Version of the Holy Bible.

SEVEN MINUTES WITH JESUS FOR MEN
Applying the Gospel of John to Everyday Life (A 60-Day Devotional)

Ray Cummings
Raycummings1970@icloud.com

ISBN: 979-8-88769-382-8
eBook ISBN: 979-8-88769-383-5
Printed in the United States of America
© 2025 by Ray Cummings

Whitaker House
1030 Hunt Valley Circle
New Kensington, PA 15068
www.whitakerhouse.com

Library of Congress Control Number: 2025902855

No part of this book may be reproduced or transmitted in any form or by any means, electronic or mechanical—including photocopying, recording, or by any information storage and retrieval system—without permission in writing from the publisher. Please direct your inquiries to permissionseditor@whitakerhouse.com.

1 2 3 4 5 6 7 8 9 10 11 ⓌⒽ 32 31 30 29 28 27 26 25

INTRODUCTION

We all have 1,440 minutes daily, meaning seven minutes is less than one percent of your daily schedule. Can seven minutes change your day? Can less than one percent of your day radically impact each day? To answer those questions, let's look at what can happen in seven minutes. An elite runner can run a mile and a half in seven minutes. Depending upon the conditions, a NASCAR driver can drive approximately twenty-one miles in seven minutes. The average jet can carry you roughly sixty-five miles in seven minutes. What can happen in seven minutes is determined by the amount of power behind you.

Is there anything or anyone more powerful than God? Absolutely not. Without question, no one or nothing is mightier than our God. What would happen if you spent seven minutes daily in God's Word? The possibilities are limitless. There is no way to determine how far God can carry you forward in that short time if you commit it daily to Him. Perhaps God could use that time to kickstart your spiritual maturity and make you more like Him.

Please don't misinterpret the title of this devotional series. I strongly encourage you to spend more than seven minutes with Jesus daily. However, seven minutes is simply the length of time it will take to read each day's devotion. Throughout your day, God will remind you of each day's Scripture and devotional thoughts as you grow in your relationship with Him. Not to mention, there is an ongoing conversation in prayer with God that is always available to every believer.

This sixty-day journey through the book of John provides a bite-size approach to Scripture in the hopes that you will carefully apply God's Word to your everyday life. Jesus practiced this same approach of smaller teaching segments with His first disciples. His longest sermon, the Sermon on the Mount, can be read in less than twelve minutes. Peter's sermon at Pentecost was less than three minutes long, and 3,000 souls were saved! (See Acts 2:14–41.) A great deal can happen briefly when that time is set apart by God and for God.

Each day is strategically built with the following framework:

- Scripture reading: a passage from the book of John.
- Key verses: verses that are vital to each day's devotion.
- Explanation: introducing key insights and biblically grounded concepts to help you grow.

- Application: thought-provoking questions for you to ponder by yourself or with others.
- Prayer: I provide a helpful prayer prompt allowing you to pray with God alone.

As we begin our study of John, let's examine two important questions.

First question: Why are there four gospels? David Guzik's commentary provides a clear answer:

> There are not four gospels, but one fourfold gospel. Each gospel presents a different perspective on the life of Jesus, and we need all four to get the complete picture.
>
> The first three gospels center on Jesus' ministry in Galilee. John centers his gospel on what Jesus said and did in Jerusalem.
>
> Each of the gospels emphasizes a different origin of Jesus. Matthew shows Jesus came from Abraham through David, and demonstrates that He is the Messiah promised in the Old Testament (Matthew 1:1–17). Mark shows Jesus came from Nazareth, demonstrating that Jesus is a Servant (Mark 1:9). Luke shows Jesus came from Adam, demonstrating that Jesus is the Perfect Man (Luke 3:23–38). John shows Jesus came from heaven, demonstrating that Jesus is God.[1]

Second question: What was the purpose of John's gospel? We find the answer in John 20:30–31:

---

1. David Guzik, *The Enduring Word Bible Commentary by David Guzik* (David Guzik, 1996), https://enduringword.com/.

> *The disciples saw Jesus do many other miraculous signs in addition to the ones recorded in this book. But these are written so that you may continue to believe that Jesus is the Messiah, the Son of God, and that by believing in him you will have life by the power of his name.*

The goal of every word written about Jesus in the Gospel of John is to help us believe in Jesus Christ. A growing faith in Jesus can lead us to find our true reason for living. So join us as we study the book of John to strengthen our faith and find life in Jesus's name.

Day 1

SCRIPTURE READING: JOHN 1:1–18

Key Verses: John 1:1–2, 4–5, 14, 16

In the beginning the Word already existed. The Word was with God, and the Word was God. He existed in the beginning with God.

The Word gave life to everything that was created, and his life brought light to everyone. The light shines in the darkness, and the darkness can never extinguish it.

So the Word became human and made his home among us. He was full of unfailing love and faithfulness. And we have seen his glory, the glory of the Father's one and only Son.

From his abundance we have all received one gracious blessing after another.

Explanation:

Thank you for joining us in this devotional study of the book of John. Matthew and Luke start with the birth of Christ. Mark begins with John the Baptist preparing the way for Jesus. However, John jumps straight into the deep end and begins with Jesus's eternal nature. Jesus is the Word, and He has always existed. (It helps me understand reading John 1 by replacing "Word" with "Jesus.") Not only is Jesus timeless, but He was always with God, and He is always God. Talk about mind-blowing information to begin a book! I believe John is trying to convey that Jesus is incomprehensible.

Let me see if I can illustrate. Some of you, like me, may have spent years chasing that elusive ten-point buck. Year after year, you hunted him until finally, one day, he made a mistake and stepped out in front of your stand. He has been on your wall now for years, and the excitement you once felt while chasing him has faded.

Maybe you spent years saving money to buy that truck you always wanted. You were finally able to purchase it, and you loved it for a while. Now, the new scent has faded, replaced by other odors. Remember that chasing after the things of this world never satisfies.

However, a relationship with Jesus satisfies us completely. The magnitude of His nature is incomprehensible, igniting a desire to seek and know Him further. A relationship with Jesus should never grow dull or boring. We should stand in awe of Him because of who He is and always show gratitude to Him because of all He does.

John describes Jesus in this opening chapter in the following ways:

- Jesus is eternal and has no beginning or end. (See John 1:1–2.)
- He is the Word, meaning Jesus speaks to us. (See John 1:1.)
- He is with God, and He is God! Here, the triune nature of God is disclosed, even though our words can never honestly explain it. (See John 1:1.)

- In Him is Life. (See John 1:4.)
- Through Jesus is Light. (See John 1:4–5, 9.)
- He took on flesh and made His home among us. (See John 1:14.)
- From His abundance comes our every blessing. (See John 1:16.)

Application:

How do you find your deepest fulfillment and satisfaction in a relationship with a God who is inconceivable in greatness?

Prayer:

God, nothing in this world brings lasting satisfaction but You. Our gratification and joy increase the more we know You. Please help me in this journey through John to get a greater glimpse of who You are....

Day 2

SCRIPTURE READING: JOHN 1:19–34

Key Verses: John 1:29–34

> *The next day John saw Jesus coming toward him and said, "Look! The Lamb of God who takes away the sin of the world! He is the one I was talking about when I said, 'A man is coming after me who is far greater than I am, for he existed long before me.' I did not recognize him as the Messiah, but I have been baptizing with water so that he might be revealed to Israel."*
>
> *Then John testified, "I saw the Holy Spirit descending like a dove from heaven and resting upon him. I didn't know he was the one, but when God sent me to baptize with water, he told me, 'The one on whom you see the Spirit descend and rest is the one who will baptize with the Holy Spirit.' I saw this happen to Jesus, so I testify that he is the Chosen One of God."*

Explanation:

If you searched the web for a definition of "testify," you would find these words: "To make a statement based on personal knowledge or belief; bear witness; to serve as evidence or proof; or to express a personal conviction."[2] Have you ever had to testify as a witness during a trial? If you have, you know that you were sworn to tell the truth about your observations or experiences.

John the Baptist is testifying about Jesus Christ. When John the Baptist sees Jesus, he exclaims: *"Look! The Lamb of God who takes away the sin of the world!"* (John 1:29). As you read today and tomorrow's sections in the Gospel of John, you will notice that on back-to-back days John gives identical testimony about Jesus. (See John 1:35.) John is adamant that Jesus is the *"Lamb of God"* and convinced that Jesus will take away the world's sin.

The Old Testament refers to a lamb ninety-six times, with eighty-five of those occurrences signifying a sacrifice. What is also interesting is the connection John the Baptist's family has to the Old Testament sacrificial system. If you remember, John the Baptist's father, Zechariah, was a Jewish priest in the temple of Jerusalem. (See Luke 1:5–25). He was actually in the sanctuary doing his priestly duties when God showed him that John the Baptist would be born to his wife, Elizabeth. John the Baptist was raised in the context of the sacrificial system, making him well-acquainted with the ritual of lamb sacrifices. When John identifies Jesus as the *"Lamb of God,"* he testifies that God sent Jesus to be the final sin offering for the world.

In addition, John the Baptist and Jesus were most likely related. John the Baptist's mother, Elizabeth, and Jesus's mother, Mary, were related. Therefore, it adds to the credibility of John the Baptist's testimony that he knows Jesus

---

2. Merriam-Webster.com Dictionary, s.v. "testify," accessed February 26, 2025, https://www.merriam-webster.com/dictionary/testify.

personally and understands what the sacrifice of lambs signifies. John the Baptist is an eyewitness testimony to lambs and the Lord. Knowing this, he confirms that Jesus is God's Son. He is sure that Jesus's sacrifice will solve our sin problem!

Application:

Are you convinced that Jesus is the *"Lamb of God who takes away the sin of the world?"*(John 1:29). In what ways are you a witness for Him?

Prayer:

Lamb of God, thank You for sacrificing Your life to take away my sin. Help me be strong enough to testify boldly that Jesus, You are the Son of God....

Day 3

SCRIPTURE: JOHN 1:35–50

Key Verses: John 1:35–41

The following day John was again standing with two of his disciples. As Jesus walked by, John looked at him and declared, "Look! There is the Lamb of God!" When John's two disciples heard this, they followed Jesus.

Jesus looked around and saw them following. "What do you want?" he asked them.

They replied, "Rabbi" (which means "Teacher"), "where are you staying?"

"Come and see," he said. It was about four o'clock in the afternoon when they went with him to the place where he was staying, and they remained with him the rest of the day.

Andrew, Simon Peter's brother, was one of these men who heard what John said and then followed Jesus. Andrew went to find his brother, Simon, and told him, "We have found the Messiah" (which means "Christ").

Explanation:

When John the Baptist announced a second time that Jesus was the Lamb of God, two disciples stopped following John the Baptist and started following Jesus. The first name these disciples called Jesus was Rabbi, which means "teacher." To follow Jesus, we must submit ourselves to a student/teacher relationship. Jesus is the Master Teacher. He instructs us as we listen and learn.

This is what it means to be a disciple of Jesus. "Disciple" comes from the Greek word *mathétés* in the New Testament. The Greek root word is *math*, which means "the mental effort needed to think something through."[3] In its simplest form, it means a learner. To disciple someone means to help someone progressively learn the Word of God and practically live it out daily.

God wants to help you learn what it means to grow as a Christian. As you follow His example, Jesus will teach you to become more like Him.

When Andrew found his brother, Simon, he told him, *"'We have found the Messiah,' which means 'Christ'"* (John 1:41). It didn't take Andrew long to learn that Jesus was the Christ, the long-awaited Messiah.

Teacher and Christ are two valuable names for Jesus. He is our Master Teacher and our Messiah. Jesus comes to save us and invites us on a life-long journey to grow as one of His disciples.

More people like the saving nature of Jesus than the teaching aspect. However, when Jesus saves us, then the learning really begins. That is why Jesus refers to salvation as being *"born again."* (See John 3:3, 7.)

---

3. "3101. Mathétés," HELPS Word-studies, Discovery Bible, accessed February 27, 2025, https://biblehub.com/greek/3101.htm.

Fathers know that once a child is born, a long journey of growth and learning begins. It takes years for children to develop and mature by listening to and learning from their parents. When Jesus saves you and adopts you into His family, it will also take years of learning for you to mature as a follower of Christ.

Application:

Jesus wants every saved child to become His disciple. How are you listening, learning, growing, and maturing as a follower of Jesus Christ?

Prayer:

Jesus, thank You for being my Messiah and Master Teacher. Help me to follow You daily and grow to become all that You desire me to be....

Day 4

SCRIPTURE: JOHN 2:1–12

Key Verses: John 2:1–3, 5, 7–10

> The next day there was a wedding celebration in the village of Cana in Galilee. Jesus' mother was there, and Jesus and his disciples were also invited to the celebration. The wine supply ran out during the festivities, so Jesus' mother told him, "They have no more wine." ...
>
> His mother told the servants, "Do whatever he tells you."...
>
> Jesus told the servants, "Fill the jars with water." When the jars had been filled, he said, "Now dip some out, and take it to the master of ceremonies." So the servants followed his instructions.
>
> When the master of ceremonies tasted the water that was now wine, not knowing where it had come from (though, of course, the servants knew), he called the bridegroom over. "A host always serves the best wine first," he said. "Then, when everyone has had a lot to drink, he brings out the less expensive wine. But you have kept the best until now!"

Explanation:

Some people tend to think that God is boring. Nothing could be further from the truth! Jesus's first public miracle was at a wedding celebration. Jesus enjoyed celebrating. Since Christ is life (see John 14:6), only Jesus can bring true life to the party!

It is all too common for people to include Jesus in a religious ceremony yet leave Him out of their daily lives. This miracle showed that Jesus cared about marriage. Not only should we invite Jesus to our weddings, but it is essential that we extend Him an invitation to our marriages.

The wedding host ran into a humiliating scenario of running out of wine at the celebration. Mary knew her son and His disciples were in attendance and informed Jesus of the dilemma.

How often do we try to solve our problems in our strength before bringing them to Jesus? Mary understood that the larger the issue, the quicker it should be brought to Jesus. So, she immediately told Jesus, *"They have no more wine"* (John 2:3).

Mary sent servants with Jesus, saying, *"Do whatever he tells you"* (John 2:5). How much better would our lives be if we sought out Jesus at the first signs of trouble and obeyed His commands?

The servants followed Jesus's order and filled six ceremonial water jars with about twenty to thirty gallons each. Then He told them to dip some out and take it to the master of ceremonies. The master of ceremonies tasted the wine, but didn't know where it came from. He complimented the bridegroom on saving the best wine until last. The obedient servants who followed Jesus had a front-row seat to Jesus's first miracle. They understood what few people at the party knew. When we stay close to Jesus, we will be privy to God's wonder-working power.

The statement from the master of ceremonies is profound: *"'A host always serves the best wine first,' he said. 'Then, when everyone has had a lot to drink, he brings out the less expensive wine'"* (John 2:10). The cheap wine comes out last at most parties because the people are too wayward to realize what they are drinking by then. However, Jesus saved the best for last! Realize that no matter how difficult life gets, an eternal party awaits us in heaven. Every moment spent with Jesus will be worth it when you attend the marriage supper of the Lamb! (See Revelation 19:6–9.)

Application:

Will you obey whatever God tells you to do, knowing He has good things in store for you?

Prayer:

God, thank You for bringing true life to the party! Please teach me how to live joyfully, knowing You save the best until last....

Day 5

SCRIPTURE: JOHN 2:13–22

Key Verses: John 2:13–15, 18–22

It was nearly time for the Jewish Passover celebration, so Jesus went to Jerusalem. In the Temple area he saw merchants selling cattle, sheep, and doves for sacrifices; he also saw dealers at tables exchanging foreign money. Jesus made a whip from some ropes and chased them all out of the Temple....

But the Jewish leaders demanded, "What are you doing? If God gave you authority to do this, show us a miraculous sign to prove it."

"All right," Jesus replied. "Destroy this temple, and in three days I will raise it up."

"What!" they exclaimed. "It has taken forty-six years to build this Temple, and you can rebuild it in three days?" But when Jesus said "this temple," he meant his own body. After he was raised from the dead, his disciples remembered he had said this, and they believed both the Scriptures and what Jesus had said.

Explanation:

Have you ever been misunderstood? I'm sure we have all been misinterpreted multiple times in our lives. The next time somebody misunderstands what you are attempting to convey, realize that you are in good company because Jesus was often misunderstood, too.

In today's passage of Scripture, Jesus displayed His righteous anger at merchants who had turned a place of worship into a profit center. In biblical times, people brought a spotless animal as a sacrifice to God for their sins. The religious leaders had wickedly devised a plan to make some extra money from people who had traveled for weeks to worship. They told the traveling worshippers that the sacrifice they brought was not good enough and sold them ones they had deemed sufficient at outrageous prices. Money changers also exchanged foreign currency at higher fees to exploit worshippers.

So Jesus, with divine self-control, took time to make a whip and ran the swindlers out of the Temple courts. I believe many misinterpreted Jesus's judgment of their sins as merely an angry reaction. Yet, the Bible assures us that Jesus was sinless; His reaction was a direct response to God's house being turned *"into a marketplace"* (John 2:16).

The Jewish leaders became upset at Jesus's actions and questioned His authority. (See John 2:18.) Can you imagine religious hypocrites distrusting the authority of Jesus Christ? These self-titled religious leaders demanded that Jesus give them a sign that He had God's authority. In response, Jesus declared, *"Destroy this temple, and in three days I will raise it up"* (John 2:19). The leaders misunderstood Jesus so much that they did the math and told Jesus that it took forty-six years to build the temple.

This passage indicates that the religious leaders overlooked God's message, and His disciples only understood it after Jesus's death and resurrection. The Bible clarifies that Jesus referred to His own body rather than the temple. Jesus had just declared that He would die and God would raise Him up in three days. This was the greatest news that would ever be announced, and the religious elite of their day completely missed it!

Application:

How often do you miss what God is trying to say in His Word? Please don't feel bad because it happens to all of us. Just know that if you keep following Jesus long enough, He will reveal the truth behind every word He speaks.

Prayer:

God, when I am misunderstood, help me think about You. I know You understand how I feel when people judge me and misunderstand my words and actions. Please help me walk by faith, knowing that You will teach me Your truths progressively as I continue to follow You....

Day 6

SCRIPTURE: JOHN 2:23–3:8

Key Verses: John 3:1–7

There was a man named Nicodemus, a Jewish religious leader who was a Pharisee. After dark one evening, he came to speak with Jesus. "Rabbi," he said, "we all know that God has sent you to teach us. Your miraculous signs are evidence that God is with you."

Jesus replied, "I tell you the truth, unless you are born again, you cannot see the Kingdom of God."

"What do you mean?" exclaimed Nicodemus. "How can an old man go back into his mother's womb and be born again?"

Jesus replied, "I assure you, no one can enter the Kingdom of God without being born of water and the Spirit. Humans can reproduce only human life, but the Holy Spirit gives birth to spiritual life. So don't be surprised when I say, 'You must be born again.'"

Explanation:

Yesterday, we mentioned that people often misunderstand Jesus. In John 3, we find yet another extremely religious man who, at first, misinterpreted what Jesus was trying to say. His name was Nicodemus. Here is what Scripture tells us about his religious credentials. He was a Jew, a Pharisee, and a member of the Sanhedrin, which put him in the top seventy religious scholars of his day. Ironically, the name Nicodemus means "victory of the people."[4]

Nicodemus had heard about Jesus's miracles and teachings. In the depths of his heart, he wanted to know more about Christ. He met Jesus one evening when no one would see them. Nicodemus had his reputation to uphold, but deep in his soul, he knew that Jesus could be the Messiah.

Nicodemus started the conversation with a general statement. *"'Rabbi,' he said, 'we all know that God has sent you to teach us. Your miraculous signs are evidence God is with you'"* (John 3:2). Jesus turned the conversation from miracles to the moment of salvation. Jesus said, *"I tell you the truth, unless you are born again you cannot see the Kingdom of God"* (John 3:3).

Nicodemus, an elite religious scholar, thought Jesus was referring to physical birth. However, Jesus was speaking of a spiritual birth. Every human being who ever lived was born physically. Yet only those who trust Jesus Christ as Lord and Savior can be born spiritually—*"born again."* God sent His Son Jesus to give every person with a physical birthday an opportunity to have a spiritual birth.

Did Nicodemus ever make sense out of what Jesus was teaching him? I believe so. He aided Joseph of Arimathea, a secret disciple of Jesus, in removing Jesus's body from the cross and preparing it for burial. John 19:39 says, *"With him [Joseph of Arimathea] came Nicodemus, the man who had come to Jesus at night."* It is as if God wants us to know that

---

4. "3530. Nikodēmos," Bible Hub, accessed February 27, 2025, https://biblehub.com/greek/3530.htm.

this is the same Nicodemus mentioned in John 3. Remember, it matters most not how you start but how you finish!

Application:

If you have ever struggled with questions about trusting Jesus Christ, Nicodemus knows exactly how you feel. Keep asking Jesus your questions because He is the One who has all the answers.

Prayer:

Lord, I want to finish well when it comes to putting my faith in You. Help me not to be a secret disciple, but to publicly demonstrate my love for You as Nicodemus did....

Day 7

SCRIPTURE READING: JOHN 3:9–21

Key Verses: John 3:13–17

> *No one has ever gone to heaven and returned. But the Son of Man has come down from heaven. And as Moses lifted up the bronze snake on a pole in the wilderness, so the Son of Man must be lifted up, so that everyone who believes in him will have eternal life.*
>
> *For this is how God loved the world: He gave his one and only Son, so that everyone who believes in him will not perish but have eternal life. God sent his Son into the world not to judge the world, but to save the world through him.*

Explanation:

In the course of discussing salvation with Nicodemus, Jesus makes the most well-known statement in all of Scripture—John 3:16.

> *For God so loved the world that he gave his one and only Son, that whoever believes in him shall not perish but have eternal life.* (John 3:16 NIV)

There are two different thoughts on interpreting the word "so" in John 3:16. Some believe that the word "so" refers to the extent of God's love for the world. That's how the *New International Version* interprets it, as does *The Message*, which reads: *"This is how much God loved the world: He gave his Son, his one and only Son."*

The second interpretation of the word "so" means the manner in which God loved the world. This is how the *New Living Translation* states it: *"For this is how God loved the world: He gave his one and only Son, so that everyone who believes in him will not perish but have eternal life."* Most scholars believe this interpretation is more accurate because the New Testament word "so" actually means "in this manner."

If this is the case, many Christians have grown up not realizing the full implications of John 3:16. When we read John 3:16 and hear it preached, the focus is often immediately on us. Yes, God loves us. Yet, the focus is on God, not us. We are not so valuable that God loves us; God loves us, making us so valuable. This brings a significant change in the way people think about themselves and God. Many individuals think highly of themselves, leading them to rely on God less than they should, or not at all. They may think, "I'm a great person, and God loves me." Instead, we should have this mindset: "God loves me, so this gives me the potential to be great."

When we read, *"This is how God loved the world,"* our attention properly focuses on God. God's love is selfless, gracious, boundless, and endless. God did not love us because He needed us. We need God's love and will never understand our true purpose for living without it. We have the potential to be saved and forgiven of our sins because God's love is so great that He sent His only Son to die in our place. No one is worthy of God's love. It wasn't our worth that caused Jesus to die; it was God sending His Son that allowed us to live worthy lives.

This truth will be expounded on tomorrow when we see John the Baptist's humility in the presence of Jesus Christ. John realized that *"No one can receive anything unless God gives it from heaven"* (John 3:27). More about that tomorrow, but let's make today and every day about Jesus!

Application:

How can you focus on God's love, which gives you worth so that you continually depend on Him?

Prayer:

God, thank You for having a love so great that You would send Your Son to die for me. Help me always remember that my true worth and value come through You....

Day 8

SCRIPTURE READING: JOHN 3:22–36

Key Verses: John 3:27–30

> John replied, "No one can receive anything unless God gives it from heaven. You yourselves know how plainly I told you, 'I am not the Messiah. I am only here to prepare the way for him.' It is the bridegroom who marries the bride, and the bridegroom's friend is simply glad to stand with him and hear his vows. Therefore, I am filled with joy at his success. He must become greater and greater, and I must become less and less.'"

Explanation:

John the Baptist is the perfect example of the humility required to live a life that points people to Jesus. Remember that it was John the Baptist who three times pointed to Jesus as the Lamb of God who would take away the world's sins. When Jesus stepped onto the scene in human history, John the Baptist was a well-known leader with his own followers. Yet when Jesus entered the picture, John immediately stepped into the shadows and gave room for Jesus to stand in the spotlight. John the Baptist even had followers leave him and follow Jesus instead. Not once in Scripture will you find John the Baptist upset because Jesus was getting recognized.

In fact, John the Baptist's purpose for living was to bring glory to Jesus Christ.

In John 3:28, John the Baptist reminds his followers of how often he told them he was not the Messiah and that he existed only to prepare the way for Him. In John 3:29, John the Baptist describes living a life surrendered to the lordship of Christ by using this excellent wedding analogy: *"It is the bridegroom who marries the bride, and the bridegroom's friend is simply glad to stand with him and hear his vows."* Jesus is the bridegroom, and His church is the bride. Jesus died for the church so that the church could be joined together with Him. John the Baptist described himself as merely the bridegroom's friend and said that he was glad to stand with Jesus and listen to His vows to His church. He reiterates his purpose and pleasure with these words: *"Therefore, I am filled with joy at his success"* (John 3:29).

In today's me-centered society, it isn't easy to genuinely wish others success. Too often, we make life about us and focus only on ourselves. John the Baptist gives a refreshing example and reminder that God gave us this life so that we could bring glory to Him.

In John 3:30, John the Baptist gives what I believe is his life's purpose statement: *"He must become greater and greater, and I must become less and less."* Less of me provides more room in my heart for Jesus. For God's greatness to fill my life, I need to decrease, and He needs to increase!

Application:
How are you tempted to make life about you? In what ways do you need to become less so that Jesus can become greater?

Prayer:

Please help me, Lord, to find the most genuine joy in seeing You glorified. In this world, I am often tempted to make life about myself. Help me decrease so that you can increase. Grant me genuine fulfillment in standing next to You, the Bridegroom, as You lead Your bride, the church....

Day 9

SCRIPTURE READING: JOHN 4:1–14

Key Verses: John 4:7–14

Soon a Samaritan woman came to draw water, and Jesus said to her, "Please give me a drink." He was alone at the time because his disciples had gone into the village to buy some food.

The woman was surprised, for Jews refuse to have anything to do with Samaritans. She said to Jesus, "You are a Jew, and I am a Samaritan woman. Why are you asking me for a drink?"

Jesus replied, "If you only knew the gift God has for you and who you are speaking to, you would ask me, and I would give you living water."

"But sir, you don't have a rope or a bucket," she said, "and this well is very deep. Where would you get this living water? And besides, do you think you're greater than our ancestor Jacob, who gave us this well? How can you offer better water than he and his sons and his animals enjoyed?"

Jesus replied, "Anyone who drinks this water will soon become thirsty again. But those who drink the water

I give will never be thirsty again. It becomes a fresh, bubbling spring within them, giving them eternal life."

Explanation:

There are two things that all people have in common: We all have sinned against God, and we all have something in our past we would like to forget. As we begin today's devotion, think about this one question: How many barriers has Jesus broken down in your life to bring you to Himself?

In John 4, we read the account of Jesus Christ meeting a Samaritan woman at noon one day at a well. Jesus broke through four huge barriers in this encounter. (We will look at two today and save the final two for tomorrow's devotion.)

First, Jesus broke down the barrier of gender. In biblical times, men (especially rabbis) did not associate with women publicly (especially alone). Yet, Jesus treated this woman with dignity and respect. Jesus elevated the status of women from the world's distorted view to a biblical one: *"There is neither male nor female; for you are all one in Christ Jesus"* (Galatians 3:28 NKJV).

Second, Jesus broke through the obstacle of how people view ethnicity. At the time of this meeting, Jews and Samaritans despised each other. The Jews considered Samaritans to be of illegitimate ancestry and later even used the word "Samaritan" as an insult towards Jesus. (In John 8:48, people called Jesus *"You Samaritan devil!"*) Jesus faced the ugly insults made by people who want to make ethnicity an issue. However, Jesus, a Jew, treated everyone equally, including this Samaritan woman in John 4.

One day, every knee will bow, and every tongue will confess that Jesus is Lord. (See Romans 14:11 and Philippians

2:10–11.) One day, there will be a great multitude that no one can count, *"from every nation and tribe and people and language,"* standing before the throne and before the Lamb (Revelation 7:9). A day will come when all the barriers humans have created between one another are eliminated by Jesus, our Lord.

Application:

Since Jesus sees no barriers between genders and races, how should we live as His followers?

Prayer:

Thank You for seeing all people the same and demonstrating it in Your love for the Samaritan woman at the well. Please help me not to build barriers in places where You have taken them down....

Day 10

SCRIPTURE READING: JOHN 4:15–26

Key Verses: John 4:15–19, 25–26

> *"Please, sir," the woman said, "give me this water! Then I'll never be thirsty again, and I won't have to come here to get water."*
>
> *"Go and get your husband," Jesus told her.*
>
> *"I don't have a husband," the woman replied.*
>
> *Jesus said, "You're right! You don't have a husband—for you have had five husbands, and you aren't even married to the man you're living with now. You certainly spoke the truth!"*
>
> *"Sir," the woman said, "you must be a prophet."…*
>
> *The woman said, "I know the Messiah is coming—the one who is called Christ. When he comes, he will explain everything to us."*
>
> *Then Jesus told her, "I AM the Messiah!"*

Explanation:

Yesterday, we discussed Jesus breaking down the barriers of gender and ethnicity. As we continue to read about Jesus's encounter with the woman at the well, we notice that He has broken down two more barriers.

In John 4:15–19, Jesus overcame the third barrier, breaking down the wall of her past. It is interesting to note how Jesus gets her to confess her past. Knowing everything, Jesus tells her to go and get her husband. The woman is honest and says, *"I don't have a husband."* Jesus confronts her with the fact that she answered correctly, but in reality, she has been married five times and is currently living with a man who isn't her husband. Talk about bringing up somebody's past!

Why would Jesus do that? So He could save her from her past and give her a brand-new future! When we confess our sins, He faithfully forgives us and cleanses us of all unrighteousness. (See 1 John 1:9.) (I am so glad that Jesus broke down the barriers of my past and brought me to Himself!)

The last barrier Jesus broke through with the woman at the well was the barrier of religion (John 4:19–24). The Samaritans worshipped on a mountain called Gerizim because that's where their ancestors worshipped. Many Jews thought that Jerusalem was the only actual place for worship. Jesus broke through the false religious idea that worship was confined to a place. Instead, Jesus taught that worship was about Father God and was done in spirit and truth. (See John 4:24.) We often tend to make worship about us, our opinions, and preferences. True worship is about the sincerity of our hearts and is focused on the truth of who God is.

After all these four barriers were shattered, Jesus told her why He could break down every barrier in her life. He said, *"I AM the Messiah!"* (John 4:26). Jesus not only died to save us from our sins, but He also came to break down every barrier in our lives!

Application:

What barriers has Jesus broken down in your past? What obstacles of religion do you still struggle with that keep you from worshipping God in spirit and truth?

Prayer:

Thank You for being a barrier-breaking God. Help me to trust in Your power to destroy anything that seeks to separate me from You....

Day 11

SCRIPTURE READING: JOHN 4:27–38

Key Verses: John 4:27, 31–35

> *Just then his disciples came back. They were shocked to find him talking to a woman, but none of them had the nerve to ask,…"Why are you talking to her?"…*
>
> *Meanwhile, the disciples were urging Jesus, "Rabbi, eat something."*
>
> *But Jesus replied, "I have a kind of food you know nothing about."*
>
> *"Did someone bring him food while we were gone?" the disciples asked each other.*
>
> *Then Jesus explained: "My nourishment comes from doing the will of God, who sent me, and from finishing his work. You know the saying, 'Four months between planting and harvest.' But I say, wake up and look around. The fields are already ripe for harvest."*

Explanation:

Jesus's disciples were shocked to find Him speaking with a Samaritan woman at the well. These first followers of Jesus still had barriers that needed to be addressed. Even though they were amazed at what they saw, not one of the disciples had the nerve to ask Jesus about it.

Like many of us, they changed the subject since they were unsure what to say. The disciples grabbed something to eat on their journey, and they advised Jesus to eat something. However, Jesus changed the subject on His disciples and said, *"I have a kind of food you know nothing about"* (John 4:32). Jesus would tell them that His sustenance came from doing God's will. While His disciples were focused on food for their stomachs, Jesus was focused on a harvest of souls.

Jesus sought to awaken His disciples to the spiritual harvest around them. He admonished them to *"wake up and look around"* (verse 35). The harvest was ready; they just weren't aware or searching for it.

They were shocked that Jesus was witnessing to a Samaritan woman. Jesus was wondering why they weren't more focused on her soul than on her gender or ethnicity. The disciples were hung up on the physical while Jesus was focused on the spiritual. If Jesus found His fulfillment in seeing lost people saved, shouldn't His followers find their satisfaction in the same place?

How often do we miss the harvest of souls because we are too busy worrying about satisfying the hunger in our stomachs? It is easy to put our most significant emphasis on feeding and providing for our families' physical needs, so we tend to neglect their spiritual ones. The most critical provision we can give those around us is an opportunity to know Jesus Christ and grow in their walk with Him.

Application:

How can your spiritual focus begin with the harvest closest to you? Ask God to help you get to where you can genuinely say, *"My nourishment comes from doing the will of God"* (John 4:34).

Prayer:

God, please give me a greater hunger to see lost people saved. Awaken my spirit and open my eyes to the people around me who are ready for harvest. Help me to find my proper sustenance in accomplishing Your will for my life....

Day 12

SCRIPTURE READING: JOHN 4:39–54

Key Verses: John 4:39, 46–53

> Many Samaritans from the village believed in Jesus because the woman had said, "He told me everything I ever did!"...
>
> As he traveled through Galilee, he came to Cana, where he had turned the water into wine. There was a government official in nearby Capernaum whose son was very sick.
>
> When he heard that Jesus had come from Judea to Galilee, he went and begged Jesus to come to Capernaum to heal his son, who was about to die.
>
> Jesus asked, "Will you never believe in me unless you see miraculous signs and wonders?"
>
> The official pleaded, "Lord, please come now before my little boy dies."
>
> Then Jesus told him, "Go back home. Your son will live!" And the man believed what Jesus said and started home.
>
> While the man was on his way, some of his servants met him with the news that his son was alive and well. He asked them when the boy had begun to get better,

and they replied, "Yesterday afternoon at one o'clock his fever suddenly disappeared!" Then the father realized that that was the very time Jesus had told him, "Your son will live." And he and his entire household believed in Jesus.

Explanation:

Jesus had just encouraged His disciples to wake up and acknowledge the spiritual harvest around them. Now, they will get two first-hand and up-close looks at souls being saved.

The woman at the well told people about Jesus, and many Samaritans from the village put their faith in Him as Messiah. Jesus stayed with them for two days so that many more could hear His message and be saved. Remember, Jesus had just told His disciples that they would harvest where they didn't plant (John 4:38). They already saw this occur when they witnessed these Samaritans being saved.

Upon leaving the Samaritan village, the disciples would get another look at the spiritual harvest. A government official approached Jesus and begged Him to come to Capernaum to heal his son, who was at the point of death. Jesus told him to go back home and that his son would live. The man believed in Jesus and headed for home. Before he could arrive, he was met by some of his servants who told him the fantastic news that his boy was alive and well. They did the math and figured out that the boy was healed at the exact time when Jesus had told him that his boy would live.

John 4:54 states, *"This was the second miraculous sign Jesus did in Galilee after coming from Judea."* The first miracle was when Jesus turned the water into wine at the wedding feast. Now, these were not the only two miracles that occurred so far. John states that these were the first two miracles that were signs. The New Testament word for "signs" in this verse means "something given especially to confirm or authenticate." These two miracles confirmed that Jesus was the Christ.

However, the greatest miracle is when Jesus forgives our sins and saves us. The disciples saw much more than miraculous signs; they saw the miracle of the harvest of souls.

Application:

What does it say about Jesus that what He teaches, He also illustrates? How does this help you trust Him more and live out what He calls you to do?

Prayer:

I believe that Your greatest miracle is saving someone who is lost. Help me to keep the spiritual harvest first in my prayers and primary in my focus....

Day 13

SCRIPTURE READING: JOHN 5:1–15

Key Verses: John 5:1–9

> *Afterward Jesus returned to Jerusalem for one of the Jewish holy days. Inside the city, near the Sheep Gate, was the pool of Bethesda, with five covered porches. Crowds of sick people—blind, lame, or paralyzed—lay on the porches.*
>
> *One of the men lying there had been sick for thirty-eight years. When Jesus saw him and knew he had been ill for a long time, he asked him, "Would you like to get well?"*
>
> *"I can't, sir," the sick man said, "for I have no one to put me into the pool when the water bubbles up. Someone else always gets there ahead of me."*
>
> *Jesus told him, "Stand up, pick up your mat, and walk!"*
>
> *Instantly, the man was healed! He rolled up his sleeping mat and began walking!*

Explanation:

Jerusalem was a walled city with strategically placed gates along its walls. John specifically stated that the pool of Bethesda was near the sheep gate. This gate was used to bring sheep into the temple for sacrificial offerings. It was also where animals were sold so travelers could buy a spotless animal for sacrifice. The King James Version refers to this place as the *"sheep market"* (John 5:2).

"Bethesda" is the New Testament word that means "house of mercy." The Lamb of God showed mercy to a sick man near the gate, which signified sacrifice.

Scripture gives us a detailed look at Bethesda's pool. Five covered porches surrounded the pool. Sick people would gather in the shade of these porches. When the water began moving, sick people raced to get into the pool, hoping to be healed. Bethesda was a crowded place, full of desperate and distressed sick people.

John tells us that one of the men by the pool had been sick for thirty-eight years. That amounts to nearly two thousand weeks battling a chronic illness, with a cure just beyond his reach.

Jesus knew this man's condition, singling him out of many sick people by asking, *"Would you like to get well?"* (John 15:6).

The obvious answer would be, "Of course! Yes, I want to get well!" But notice the sick man's response: *"I can't."* He didn't have anyone to help him get into the water, and someone always beat him in the race to the water.

Have you ever felt helpless and hopeless? Have you ever told yourself:

"I can't."

"I can't solve this problem."

"I can't beat this addiction."

"I can't ever get a break."

"I can't be the man God has called me to be."

That day, a man who had been sick for thirty-eight years realized that while he couldn't, God could! God doesn't need a pool to heal! Jesus told him to *"Stand up, pick up your mat, and walk!"* (John 5:8). He had been trying to get to a pool at the house of mercy all those years; all he needed to do was to meet Jesus!

Application:

How can you trust Jesus with the problems that make you feel helpless and hopeless? In what areas of your life do you need His mercy today?

Prayer:

Jesus, thank You for knowing my situation and showing me mercy. Your sacrifice as the Lamb of God allows me to be saved. Your power as the Lord of All has the potential to set me free from problems that plague me. I trust in You, Jesus, to meet me at my point of need….

Day 14

SCRIPTURE READING: JOHN 5:16–30

Key Verses: John 5:16–19, 24

> *So the Jewish leaders began harassing Jesus for breaking the Sabbath rules. But Jesus replied, "My Father is always working, and so am I." So the Jewish leaders tried all the harder to find a way to kill him. For he not only broke the Sabbath, he called God his Father, thereby making himself equal with God. So Jesus explained,…*
>
> *"I tell you the truth, those who listen to my message and believe in God who sent me have eternal life. They will never be condemned for their sins, but they have already passed from death into life."*

Explanation:

Have you ever done the right thing for the right reason, and still, somebody fusses at you and questions your actions? You are in good company. It happened to your Savior Jesus often.

Jesus healed the man at the pool of Bethesda, but it happened to be on the Sabbath. The Jewish leaders *"began harassing Jesus for breaking the Sabbath rules"* (John 5:16). The word "harass" is also translated as "persecuted." The Greek word *dióko* means "to aggressively chase like a hunter pursuing a catch."[5] The religious leaders were constantly attempting to trap Jesus in hopes of finding some fault with Him. The problem was that Jesus is perfect and faultless, but that didn't stop these religious rule inspectors.

I love the response Jesus gives them when they give Him grief for healing on the Sabbath. He told them, *"My Father is always working, and so am I"* (John 5:17). Jesus made the Sabbath for man, not man for the Sabbath. (See Mark 2:27.) Scripture also tells us that Jesus is the Lord of the Sabbath. (See Mark 2:28.) Mankind needs a day of rest, but God is always working. Since Jesus is Lord over the Sabbath, He can do whatever He chooses because everything belongs to Him. (See Psalm 24:1.)

Rather than listen for something to help them trust God more, these religious leaders found something else to complain about. All they heard Jesus say was, *"My Father is always working,"* and they immediately found more fault with Jesus because He had called God His Father. Now, Jesus has claimed to be equal with God, and these leaders now want Him dead.

If they had listened to the truth in Jesus's words, they might have discovered He was indeed the Messiah they had long awaited. When you only want something to complain about, it is extremely difficult to see the truth. These men can't see the good even in Jesus Christ!

Jesus summarizes the only solution for their deceived hearts: *"I tell you the truth, those who listen to my message and believe in God who sent me have eternal life"* (John 5:24). If

---

5. "1377. dióko," Bible Hub, accessed March 3, 2025, https://biblehub.com/greek/1377.htm.

they would listen and believe, they would find salvation in Jesus Christ. Then Jesus adds, *"They will never be condemned for their sins, but they have already passed from death into life"* (John 5:24). These religious men were trying to condemn Jesus while He was trying to save them from the condemnation of their sins!

Application:

How does a condemning spirit lead to your condemnation? How does Jesus's response show His patience, love, and mercy?

Prayer:

Please Lord, take away my negative spirit and help me to listen to You and believe. Thank You for being patient with my condemning ways. Please remind me that You are constantly working to make me more like You....

Day 15

SCRIPTURE READING: JOHN 5:31–47

Key Verses: John 5:31–38

> *If I were to testify on my own behalf, my testimony would not be valid. But someone else is also testifying about me, and I assure you that everything he says about me is true. In fact, you sent investigators to listen to John the Baptist, and his testimony about me was true. Of course, I have no need of human witnesses, but I say these things so you might be saved. John was like a burning and shining lamp, and you were excited for a while about his message. But I have a greater witness than John—my teachings and my miracles. The Father gave me these works to accomplish, and they prove that he sent me. And the Father who sent me has testified about me himself. You have never heard his voice or seen him face to face, and you do not have his message in your hearts, because you do not believe me—the one he sent to you.*

Explanation:

Yesterday, we read that Jesus claimed to be the Messiah sent by God, His Father, to save people from their sins. (See John 5:17, 24–30.) Don't ever listen to anyone who says that Jesus never claimed to be God. Jesus made this claim over and over again, as recorded in His Word. So either Jesus is a liar, or He is Lord. I am convinced there is plenty of evidence that He is the latter!

In the Old Testament law, at least two to three witnesses were required to validate a claim. (See Deuteronomy 19:15.) In today's Scripture, you will discover that Jesus calls four witnesses to testify that He is indeed the Son of God.

In John 5:31–35, Jesus calls His first witness, John the Baptist. Remember that John testified twice that Jesus was the Lamb of God, who takes away the sin of the world. (See John 1:29, 36.) John affirmed that Jesus would be the final sacrifice for our sins. Every lamb ever sacrificed in the Old Testament sacrificial system pointed to one future sacrifice of God's only Son. Notice that Jesus adds the witness of John for our sake, yet also states that He doesn't need a human witness. He said, *"Of course, I have no need of human witnesses, but I say these things so you might be saved"* (John 5:34). When you meet His other three witnesses, you will see why He didn't need a human one!

In John 5:36, Jesus introduces the second witness: His teaching and miracles. Every word Jesus taught, and every miracle He performed, pointed to the power of God in His life, proving that He was indeed the Son of God. Remember when John the Baptist was later in jail and questioned whether Jesus was the Messiah, Christ sent him this message: *"Go back to John and tell him what you have heard and seen—the blind see, the lame walk, those with leprosy are cured, the deaf hear, the dead are raised to life, and the Good News is being preached to the poor"* (Matthew 11:4–5).

Jesus calls His third witness to the stand in John 5:37, God the Father. Jesus said, *"The Father who sent me has testified about me himself."* When John the Baptist baptized Jesus, God the Father spoke from heaven and said, *"This is My beloved Son, in whom I am well pleased"* (Matthew 3:17 NKJV).

The final and fourth witness is the Scriptures. Jesus declared, *"The Scriptures point to me"* (John 5:39). So Jesus is confirmed by John the Baptist, His own teachings and miracles, God the Father, and the Scriptures.

Application:

In light of all the witnesses, what would keep you from placing all your faith in Jesus as the Savior of the world?

Prayer:

Thank You, Jesus, for giving me more than I need to believe in You fully....

Day 16

SCRIPTURE READING: JOHN 6:1–15

Key Verses: John 6:5–13

Jesus soon saw a huge crowd of people coming to look for him. Turning to Philip, he asked, "Where can we buy bread to feed all these people?" He was testing Philip, for he already knew what he was going to do.

Philip replied, "Even if we worked for months, we wouldn't have enough money to feed them!"

Then Andrew, Simon Peter's brother, spoke up. "There's a young boy here with five barley loaves and two fish. But what good is that with this huge crowd?"

"Tell everyone to sit down," Jesus said. So they all sat down on the grassy slopes. (The men alone numbered about 5,000.) Then Jesus took the loaves, gave thanks to God, and distributed them to the people. Afterward he did the same with the fish. And they all ate as much as they wanted. After everyone was full, Jesus told his disciples, "Now gather the leftovers, so that nothing is wasted." So they picked up the pieces and filled twelve baskets with scraps left by the people who had eaten from the five barley loaves.

Explanation:

The feeding of the five thousand is the only miracle found in all four of the Gospels (Matthew 14:13–21; Mark 6:31–44; Luke 9:12–17; and here in John 6:1–14).

When studying Scripture, it is beneficial for biblical application to place yourself into the story by using your holy imagination. First of all, imagine being Philip when Jesus asks you where you can buy bread to feed this massive crowd of people. Scripture tells us that Jesus tested Philip because He knew He would miraculously feed them. (See John 6:6.) Philip didn't realize it was a test and failed it miserably. He figured out how much it would cost and knew that nine months of wages wouldn't even pay the bill. What would you have said if you were Philip? Would you have figured out how to solve the problem with your strength and concluded it was humanly impossible? Or would you trust the One asking you the question?

Simon Peter found a boy in the crowd with five small loaves and two fish. Now, imagine being the boy whose momma packed him lunch. It isn't your fault nobody else was prepared and brought their food. What would you have done if Jesus asked you to trust Him with your entire meal? This young boy handed Jesus everything he had and gets a front-row seat to an incredible miracle. His faith in God teaches us two truths.

First, less becomes more when you give God all that you have. God could have done the miracle with one piece of bread and half a fish. God didn't need the boy's lunch at all. He could have done the miracle without it. Yet, over five thousand people were fed from the baskets of leftovers after the boy gave all he had.

Second, less becomes more when God blesses it. At one point, the boy placed his lunch in Jesus's hands. Then Christ looked up to heaven and thanked God for it. If you put what you have in God's hands, He can bless it.

A third lesson was for all twelve disciples. They each carried the leftovers of Jesus's miracle to remind them never to doubt God!

Application:

Who can you identify with the most in this miracle: Philip, Simon Peter, this young boy who gave his lunch, or a disciple carrying his leftovers?

Prayer:

You reminded me today, Jesus, that You can provide more than I need....

Day 17

SCRIPTURE READING: JOHN 6:16–21

Key Verses: John 6:16–21

> *That evening Jesus' disciples went down to the shore to wait for him. But as darkness fell and Jesus still hadn't come back, they got into the boat and headed across the lake toward Capernaum. Soon a gale swept down upon them, and the sea grew very rough. They had rowed three or four miles when suddenly they saw Jesus walking on the water toward the boat. They were terrified, but he called out to them, "Don't be afraid. I am here!" Then they were eager to let him in the boat, and immediately they arrived at their destination!*

Explanation:

Have you ever been in turmoil and felt like Jesus was nowhere in sight? After Jesus fed the five thousand, the Gospel of Matthew tells us that He secluded Himself and prayed to the Father. (See Matthew 14:23.) John describes the event with these words: *"as darkness fell and Jesus still hadn't come back, they got into the boat and headed across the lake toward Capernaum"* (John 6:17).

Jesus left the disciples in a storm all night until shortly before dawn. (See Matthew 14:25.) The disciples rowed three to four miles in treacherous conditions and were astonished to see their Master walking on the water toward their boat around three o'clock in the morning!

It is in the trials of life that our faith is tested. God does not give you a test so He can know where you are in your faith journey. He already knows everything about you. God allows tests so that you can discover how far you've come in your walk with the Lord and how far you still have left to go. If your faith cannot be tested, how do you know it can be trusted? Amid life's storms, we spiritually grow as our faith deepens.

Jesus could have easily gotten in the boat with the disciples before the storm. However, He taught them to trust in His power, even when they could not see His presence. They were terrified when He finally showed up and thought He was a ghost. They never thought He would walk on water to get to them.

If stormwaters represented their problems, Jesus walked on them to reach His followers. No water is too deep, and no storm is too difficult to keep you away from God. He knows your situation, and He can calm your storm.

John 6:20 records Jesus's words of encouragement: *"Don't be afraid. I am here!"* We have nothing to fear, He will never abandon us. (See Hebrews 13:5.) Place your faith in His power and your confidence in His presence to find His victory over your problem.

I find John 6:21 somewhat humorous: *"Then they were eager to let him in the boat, and immediately they arrived at their destination!"* If I had been terrified while rowing a boat in a storm for several miles, I would enthusiastically invite Jesus into my problem, too! Why don't you do the same today for whatever difficulties you face? Remember that Jesus has the power to get you to the destination He has planned for you.

Application:

What storm have you been struggling with in your life? Picture Jesus walking over your problem to reach you, His child. Then, invite Him in to conquer your situation and calm your fears.

Prayer:

I am encouraged today, Lord, knowing that You know my struggles and are here to provide all the power I need. I eagerly surrender to You and earnestly invite You to exercise Your power over my problems....

Day 18

SCRIPTURE READING: JOHN 6:22–40

Key Verses: John 6:26–29, 35

> Jesus replied, "I tell you the truth, you want to be with me because I fed you, not because you understood the miraculous signs. But don't be so concerned about perishable things like food. Spend your energy seeking the eternal life that the Son of Man can give you. For God the Father has given me the seal of his approval."
>
> They replied, "We want to perform God's works, too. What should we do?"
>
> Jesus told them, "This is the only work God wants from you: Believe in the one he has sent."...
>
> "I am the bread of life. Whoever comes to me will never be hungry again. Whoever believes in me will never be thirsty."

Explanation:

Crowds were following Jesus because He had fed them with the miracle of the five loaves and two fish. Jesus knew their motives and told them they were following Him for all the wrong reasons. These people were following Him for what they could get, not to know more about who He was. The signs that Jesus performed were testimonies regarding

Jesus being the Messiah. All these people wanted was a free meal.

Some people today are just like those followers. They only come to church when there is something in it for them. Their hearts don't desire to learn more about what Scripture says about Jesus Christ. That is why a crowd doesn't necessarily connote a church. A true church is better described as a few people focused on growing their relationship with the Lord. A huge group of people who are more concerned with earthly needs than with Jesus Christ is not an accurate reflection of the church.

The false followers of Jesus's day are just as prevalent in our churches today. Many people want a miracle more than they seek a Messiah. They want a meal more than they want a Master. The followers in John 6 even ask Jesus to show them how to perform miracles. (See John 6:28.) Jesus's response is straightforward and profound: *"This is the only work God wants from you: Believe in the one he has sent"* (John 6:29). God desires for us to believe in Him much more than He wants us to seek blessings. Christ wants us to desire Him more than we hunger for our next meal. Christ knows that only He can truly satisfy the cravings of our souls.

Jesus declared, *"I am the bread of life"* (John 6:35). Christ emphasized that we will never go thirsty or hungry when we come to Him for spiritual sustenance.

As we study the Gospel of John, we often find people who followed God for the wrong reasons. Many will stop following Him when the going gets tough. As we continue this journey with Jesus, may He strengthen our commitment to follow Him with all our hearts and for all the right reasons.

Application:

Are you part of His church or the world's crowd? Since Christ already knows our motives, be honest with Him about your desire or lack of passion for Him. What distracts you from wanting more of Him in your life?

Prayer:

Lord, please instill in my heart a deep longing for You. I don't want physical blessings more than I crave a growing relationship with You. I need You, Jesus, as the bread of life....

Day 19

SCRIPTURE READING: JOHN 6:41–59

Key Verses: John 6:41–43, 47–51

Then the people began to murmur in disagreement because he had said, "I am the bread that came down from heaven." They said, "Isn't this Jesus, the son of Joseph? We know his father and mother. How can he say, 'I came down from heaven'?"

But Jesus replied, "Stop complaining about what I said....

"I tell you the truth, anyone who believes has eternal life. Yes, I am the bread of life! Your ancestors ate manna in the wilderness, but they all died. Anyone who eats the bread from heaven, however, will never die. I am the living bread that came down from heaven. Anyone who eats this bread will live forever; and this bread, which I will offer so the world may live, is my flesh."

Explanation:

In John 6:26–59, Jesus preached the great news that He is the bread of life. Looking back on His message, we receive the joy of knowing that Jesus provides the eternal sustenance and satisfaction we need. However, for most of the original hearers of this discourse, it was a sharp rebuke.

Interestingly, most churches today will do anything to attract crowds. Yet Jesus preached His harshest sermons when He had drawn the largest crowds. It was as if He was weeding out those following Him for the wrong reasons so He could teach the good news to those who genuinely believed in Him with the right motives.

In this message, Jesus described how people can be saved and why most people in the crowd wouldn't be saved. His sermon angered most of the people that day, and many of them joined the ever-increasing crowd who were planning His death.

In verses 41–42, we read that many of them did not recognize that Jesus was the Son of God. Most of them knew Jesus's earthly father and mother, so they couldn't fathom how He came down from heaven as the Messiah. Interestingly, they missed that He was the Messiah because He didn't come as they expected.

However, they believed He was the Messiah when He fed the five thousand. So when they were seeking literal bread, they thought He was the Messiah, but when He started talking about spiritual things, they now questioned whether He is the Son of God. How ironic that they missed the eternal God they had long prayed for when He started speaking about eternity!

When He started talking about eating His flesh and drinking His blood (see John 6:53), the crowd turned on Him. Jesus meant they had to fully embrace His humanity and His deity to understand how He could pay the ultimate sacrifice for their sins. They sought a beautiful conquering Messiah, not a bloody surrendering Lord.

Isn't that the trouble many people still have with Jesus today? The entire world has no problem when you picture Him as a baby in a manger in Bethlehem. They have the most trouble envisioning Him on a blood-soaked cross, unrecognizable as He died for the sins of the world.

Application:

Since believing in Jesus's death, burial, and resurrection offers us life, how can you fully embrace His sacrifice?

Prayer:

Thank You for dying so that I could live. Help me to cling to Your sacrifice on the cross daily and follow You by faith....

Day 20

SCRIPTURE READING: JOHN 6:60–71

Key Verses: John 6:60–64, 66–69

> *Many of his disciples said, "This is very hard to understand. How can anyone accept it?"*
>
> *Jesus was aware that his disciples were complaining, so he said to them, "Does this offend you? Then what will you think if you see the Son of Man ascend to heaven again? The Spirit alone gives eternal life. Human effort accomplishes nothing. And the very words I have spoken to you are spirit and life. But some of you do not believe me." (For Jesus knew from the beginning which ones didn't believe, and he knew who would betray him.)...*
>
> *At this point many of his disciples turned away and deserted him. Then Jesus turned to the Twelve and asked, "Are you also going to leave?"*
>
> *Simon Peter replied, "Lord, to whom would we go? You have the words that give eternal life. We believe, and we know you are the Holy One of God."*

Explanation:

Many people never grow to become the disciples that Jesus seeks because they don't consider the cost of following Christ. Anyone can follow Jesus when the destination is heaven, and the road is full of miracles and free meals. However, following Jesus requires a soldier's training, an athlete's dedication, and a farmer's patience. (See 2 Timothy 2:3–6.) That is why many people who make a one-time decision to believe in Jesus don't maintain their daily commitment to follow Him. Please understand that nowhere does the Bible speak about making a decision for Jesus. However, God's Word repeatedly talks about making disciples. Today's Scripture is a great example of a crowd who stopped following Jesus because His message was too difficult to understand.

When Jesus heard them complaining, He directed a question to His disciples. He asked them, *"Does this offend you?"* (John 6:61). He followed that question with a second inquiry: *"Then what will you think if you see the Son of Man ascend to heaven again?"* (John 6:62). Whoever said Jesus's words are never offensive didn't read all of His message. The Sword of the Spirit, the Word of God, is an offensive weapon. (See Ephesians 6:17.) How can an offensive weapon not be offensive? If they were offended by His message, they would indeed be offended when He left them behind and ascended into Glory.

Jesus was trying to teach His faithful disciples that they would be offended, persecuted, insulted, and slandered. Most people stop following Jesus when the going gets tough because somebody lied to them and said following Jesus is easy. They never expected problems, so they doubted who God is when trouble came.

What happened to Jesus when He followed His Father's will? He was beaten, mocked, spit on, misunderstood, slandered, crucified, and placed in a borrowed grave.

The misconception is that wimpy men follow Jesus. Nothing could be further from the truth. The most challenging thing any man could ever do is to surrender to the lordship of Christ and follow God's will for their life. That's why it takes a real man to follow Jesus. Salvation is free, but discipleship costs. It is a high price, but more than worth it!

Application:

Will you follow Jesus no matter how difficult the journey, knowing that nothing compares to following Him?

Prayer:

Lord, nothing brings eternal satisfaction except following You. Help me to dedicate myself to a life surrendered to Your will because I know that one day I will receive eternal rewards....

Day 21

SCRIPTURE READING: JOHN 7:1–9

Key Verses: John 7:1–9

After this, Jesus traveled around Galilee. He wanted to stay out of Judea, where the Jewish leaders were plotting his death. But soon it was time for the Jewish Festival of Shelters, and Jesus' brothers said to him, "Leave here and go to Judea, where your followers can see your miracles! You can't become famous if you hide like this! If you can do such wonderful things, show yourself to the world!" For even his brothers didn't believe in him.

Jesus replied, "Now is not the right time for me to go, but you can go anytime. The world can't hate you, but it does hate me because I accuse it of doing evil. You go on. I'm not going to this festival, because my time has not yet come." After saying these things, Jesus remained in Galilee.

Explanation:

Have you ever thought you knew better than anyone else how something should be done? Sometimes, we need help to become better listeners and learners because we are too busy asserting our perceived dominance and control.

In John 7, we read that Jesus's brothers are trying to tell Jesus what He should do. Can you imagine trying to give Jesus advice on the decisions He should make? We do this when we follow our own will rather than His. When God tells us to do something, and we disobey, it is just like telling Him that we know better than He does what should happen. When you think about it that way, it is much wiser to follow His will since nobody knows better than Jesus what needs to happen in your life.

What's crazy about today's Scripture is that verse 5 tells us His brothers didn't believe in Him. Why would they ask Jesus to make His ministry more public if they didn't believe in Him? Were they jealous and secretly wanted to see Him fail? Or did they think He would be killed quicker if He got out of Galilee more and spent more time around those in Judea who hated Him? We can never know for sure. All we know is that they didn't believe, yet they were still trying to tell Jesus what He should do.

How can Jesus's brothers not believe in Him? They had grown up with Him and lived in Nazareth together, yet still failed to see Him as anything more than their human brother. They should have known Him the best, yet they failed to recognize who He was because of their lack of faith. If we are not careful, those of us who have grown up in church could fail to appreciate who Jesus is because we are more concerned with religion. We must never grow so comfortable in our walk with Jesus that we stop realizing His divinity and lordship.

Jesus told His brothers, "*Now is not the right time for me to go*" (John 7:6). The *New King James Version* reads, "*My time has not yet come.*" Jesus, eternal in nature, was working on a divine timetable. Jesus is never early and never late. His timing is perfect.

Jesus would never let His earthly, unbelieving brothers tell Him what He should do and when He should do it. He carries the title of Lord for a reason! There is only one God, and His name is Jesus.

Application:

Have you ever thought you knew how to live your life best? What change in attitude needs to occur so that you can continually submit to the lordship of Christ?

Prayer:

God, I know You know best, and Your timing is perfect. Help me to trust You enough to follow Your will and wait for Your timing....

Day 22

SCRIPTURE READING: JOHN 7:10–24

Key Verses: John 7:10–16

> *But after his brothers left for the festival, Jesus also went, though secretly, staying out of public view. The Jewish leaders tried to find him at the festival and kept asking if anyone had seen him. There was a lot of grumbling about him among the crowds. Some argued, "He's a good man," but others said, "He's nothing but a fraud who deceives the people." But no one had the courage to speak favorably about him in public, for they were afraid of getting in trouble with the Jewish leaders.*
>
> *Then, midway through the festival, Jesus went up to the Temple and began to teach. The people were surprised when they heard him. "How does he know so much when he hasn't been trained?" they asked.*
>
> *So Jesus told them, "My message is not my own; it comes from God who sent me."*

Explanation:

Jesus went to the festival after His brothers had left, but He stayed out of the public view and followed His Father's will. Among the crowds who were there for the festival, there was a lot of talk about Jesus. John provides this sad testimony about their conversation: No one dared to speak well of Jesus in public because they were afraid. Everyone talked about Jesus, but nobody would say anything good about Him.

Why is it that many people have no trouble talking publicly when it comes to bragging about their grandchildren or their favorite sports team, but when it comes to speaking about God's Son and who should be the most important person in our lives, we are strangely silent? How can people spread bad news faster than they share the good news of Jesus Christ? We must find the courage to speak up publicly for Jesus Christ.

Midway through the festival, when nobody spoke up for Jesus, He went to the temple and began teaching publicly. His teaching amazed the people to the extent that they asked, *"How does he know so much when he hasn't been trained?"* (John 7:15). The crowd was amazed that Jesus could interpret and explain the Scriptures without following a rabbi. Jesus did not meet the worldly qualifications of a trained teacher, yet He spoke with divine authority. Jesus explained His teaching ability: *"My message is not my own; it comes from God who sent me"* (John 7:16). Jesus knew the Author of the Scriptures personally, so He knew exactly what God was saying through His Word.

Later, in John 7:19–23, Jesus shared that because He had healed on the Sabbath, they were trying to kill Him. He compared His actions to when they circumcised their sons on the Sabbath because not to circumcise on the eighth day after birth would break the law of Moses. So it made no logical sense why Jesus couldn't heal on the Sabbath when someone needed healing.

Then, Jesus made the following summary statement: *"Look beneath the surface so you can judge correctly"* (John 7:24). When you look just at the outward appearance of things, you are prone to misjudge the intentions and attitudes of someone's heart. These people had murder in the depths of their hearts, while Jesus's heart was full of mercy.

Application:

In what ways can you speak up more for Jesus? How important is it to look past someone's outward appearance and seek to know a person's heart?

Prayer:

Lord, help me never to be ashamed of You. Give me the courage to speak up publicly for You because I love You more than anything....

Day 23

SCRIPTURE READING: JOHN 7:25–39

Key Verses: John 7:37–39

> *On the last day, the climax of the festival, Jesus stood and shouted to the crowds, "Anyone who is thirsty may come to me! Anyone who believes in me may come and drink! For the Scriptures declare, 'Rivers of living water will flow from his heart.'" (When he said "living water," he was speaking of the Spirit, who would be given to everyone believing in him. But the Spirit had not yet been given, because Jesus had not yet entered into his glory.)*

Explanation:

What happens in John 7:25–39 demonstrates Jesus's incredible teaching and perfect timing. Scripture gives us two important details about when Jesus stood up and made His profound statement: *"Anyone who believes in Me may come and drink!"* (John 7:38). First, it was the last day of the Feast of Tabernacles. Secondly, it was at the climax of the festival.

What was the Feast of Tabernacles? This is one of the three major celebrations for Jewish people, along with the Passover and the Festival of Weeks. The Feast of Tabernacles was also known as the Feast of Shelters or Booths. Scripture details this celebration in many places, including Exodus 23:16, Leviticus 23:34–43, Numbers 29:12–20, and Deuteronomy 16:13–15.

This week-long celebration began five days after the Day of Atonement. This festival commemorated the forty-year journey of the nation of Israel through the wilderness to the promised land. During this holiday week, Jews lived in shelters to simulate how their ancestors lived during their time of wilderness wandering.

Jesus will use two important parts of the Feast of Tabernacles to illustrate spiritual truths about Himself.

The first centered around the torches that the Jews carried to light candelabras located around the walls of the temple. This demonstrated that Jesus is the Light of the World.

The second significant observance involved drawing water from the pool of Siloam. A priest would dip the water from this pool and carry it to the temple, pouring it into a silver basin next to the altar.

On the last day of the feast, the high priest would go to the pool with a golden pitcher, dip it into the water, carry it back to the temple, and pour it out on the altar of sacrifice. Levites would blow their trumpets, and the crowd would shout, *"With joy you will draw water from the wells of salvation"* (Isaiah 12:3 NIV).

This is when Jesus stood up and declared that He was living water. At the perfect moment, the greatest Teacher demonstrated the fulfillment of this celebrated festival. And John even explains Jesus's teaching further by letting everyone know that Jesus was speaking about the Holy Spirit. Just as the golden pitcher was dipped into the pool of Siloam and came out filled with water, everyone who placed their trust in Jesus Christ would receive their fill of God's Holy Spirit.

Application:

How does the incredible timing make Jesus's words a perfect lesson to receive Him as Living Water?

Prayer:

Jesus, I believe your declaration, *"Anyone who believes in Me may come and drink!"* (John 7:38). Help me to draw near to You and drink, realizing that You alone can fill me with Living Water....

Day 24

SCRIPTURE READING: JOHN 7:40–53

Key Verses: John 7:40–47, 50–52

When the crowds heard him say this, some of them declared, "Surely this man is the Prophet we've been expecting." Others said, "He is the Messiah." Still others said, "But he can't be! Will the Messiah come from Galilee? For the Scriptures clearly state that the Messiah will be born of the royal line of David, in Bethlehem, the village where King David was born." So the crowd was divided about him. Some even wanted him arrested, but no one laid a hand on him.

When the Temple guards returned without having arrested Jesus, the leading priests and Pharisees demanded, "Why didn't you bring him in?"

"We have never heard anyone speak like this!" the guards responded.

"Have you been led astray, too?" the Pharisees mocked....

Then Nicodemus, the leader who had met with Jesus earlier, spoke up. "Is it legal to convict a man before he is given a hearing?" he asked.

They replied, "Are you from Galilee, too? Search the Scriptures and see for yourself—no prophet ever comes from Galilee!"

Explanation:

Even after Jesus's incredible statement as the Living Water at the climax of the Feast of Tabernacles, many people still didn't believe He was the Messiah. One barrier to their faith was that they couldn't believe in a Messiah who came from Galilee. They knew Micah prophesied that the Messiah would be born in Bethlehem. (See Micah 5:2.)

They didn't realize that, because of the census, Jesus was born in Bethlehem and later grew up in Nazareth. It is surprising that those who doubted Jesus never dared to ask Him where He was born.

When the Pharisees later ridiculed the temple guards for not arresting Jesus, Nicodemus spoke up for Jesus. Remember, this was the religious member of the Sanhedrin who had come to Jesus at night and heard Jesus say, *"No one can see the kingdom of God unless they are born again"* (John 3:3 NIV). At least Nicodemus had the courage and wherewithal to ask, *"Is it legal to convict a man before he is given a hearing?"* (John 7:51). Years before anyone said, "Innocent until proven guilty," Nicodemus realized its wisdom.

The Pharisees tried to insult Nicodemus by asking him if he was from Galilee too. Then, they demonstrate their lack of biblical knowledge by stating, *"Search the Scriptures and see for yourself—no prophet ever comes from Galilee!"* (John 7:52) These Pharisees, who prided themselves on knowing everything the Bible said, hadn't searched the Scriptures.

If they had done their homework, they would have known 2 Kings 14:25, which says:

> *Jeroboam II recovered the territories of Israel between Lebo-hamath and the Dead Sea, just as the* Lord, *the God of Israel, had promised through Jonah son of Amittai, the prophet from Gath-hepher.*

The prophet Jonah was from Gath-hepher, which was in Galilee. The Pharisees' statement was untrue. The Gospel of John records their words to reveal how the Pharisees sought every means possible to discredit Jesus as the Messiah.

Application:

Some people will take extreme measures to discredit what they don't believe. What does it say about Nicodemus that he risked everything to stand up for Jesus?

Prayer:

Jesus, keep me focused on the truth of Your Word so that I will recognize the lies from this world....

Day 25

SCRIPTURE READING: JOHN 8:1–11

Key Verses: John 8:3–11

As he was speaking, the teachers of religious law and the Pharisees brought a woman who had been caught in the act of adultery. They put her in front of the crowd.

"Teacher," they said to Jesus, "this woman was caught in the act of adultery. The law of Moses says to stone her. What do you say?"

They were trying to trap him into saying something they could use against him, but Jesus stooped down and wrote in the dust with his finger. They kept demanding an answer, so he stood up again and said, "All right, but let the one who has never sinned throw the first stone!" Then he stooped down again and wrote in the dust.

When the accusers heard this, they slipped away one by one, beginning with the oldest, until only Jesus was left in the middle of the crowd with the woman. Then Jesus stood up again and said to the woman, "Where are your accusers? Didn't even one of them condemn you?"

"No, Lord," she said.

And Jesus said, "Neither do I. Go and sin no more."

Explanation:

John provided a vital detail when the Pharisees brought a woman to Jesus who had been caught in the act of adultery. *"They were trying to trap him into saying something they could use against him"* (John 8:6). What trap could Jesus be caught in when confronted with a woman caught in sin?

Four issues are at stake here. First, Jewish law stated that a woman who committed adultery should be stoned. (See Leviticus 20:10.) Of course, this law had to be taken before a judge with credible witnesses and tried. Nevertheless, the legalistic Pharisees who showed no grace to others wanted to see if Jesus would break an Old Testament law.

The second issue is that only the Romans had the power to execute a criminal. So, if Jesus judged her by Mosaic law, He would be breaking the governmental law of the day.

The third issue, and a very important one, is that the woman's life was at stake. If the law was carried out, she would face certain death.

The fourth issue is that the love of God was at stake. If Jesus condemned the woman, He would be acting just like the Pharisees, and they could use this against His claim to be a *"friend of tax collectors and sinners"* (Matthew 11:19 NIV).

The Pharisees had indeed done their due diligence in putting Jesus in a precarious situation. Remember, they wanted to trap Jesus in something He said. Yet Jesus doesn't immediately say anything. Instead, He stoops down and begins to write in the sand. We have no idea what He wrote. Jesus's silence angered the Pharisees, so they demanded an answer. So Jesus said, *"All right, but let the one who has never sinned throw the first stone!"* (John 8:7). Now, these hypocritical Pharisees have to take their focus off of the woman's sin and look at the reality of their own. You can't do this without realizing every person is a sinner, and we would all be condemned if it were not for the grace of God.

Many rocks of condemnation were dropped that day as the Pharisees got ensnared in their own trap. We, too, should focus on our own sins rather than point out the sins of others.

Application:
Why is it significant that Jesus showed the woman grace but still told her to *"Go and sin no more"* (John 8:11)?

Prayer:
I praise You, Lord, for being full of grace and truth. (See John 1:14.) Please help me to be full of them like You….

Day 26

SCRIPTURE READING: JOHN 8:12–30

Key Verses: John 8:12–18

> *Jesus spoke to the people once more and said, "I am the light of the world. If you follow me, you won't have to walk in darkness, because you will have the light that leads to life."*
>
> *The Pharisees replied, "You are making those claims about yourself! Such testimony is not valid."*
>
> *Jesus told them, "These claims are valid even though I make them about myself. For I know where I came from and where I am going, but you don't know this about me. You judge me by human standards, but I do not judge anyone. And if I did, my judgment would be correct in every respect because I am not alone. The Father who sent me is with me. Your own law says that if two people agree about something, their witness is accepted as fact. I am one witness, and my Father who sent me is the other."*

Explanation:

Jesus makes another monumental statement about Himself while debating the Pharisees as He continues His teaching during the Feast of Tabernacles. This feast is also referred to by the word *Sukkot*, the Hebrew word for "booths" or "huts." As you recall, Jews would stay in these temporary hut-like structures as a reminder of the forty years the Jews spent traveling from Egypt to the promised land. Moving from their homes to these transitional booths for the festival reminded them that life was frail and worldly things were temporary. The same God that directed their forefathers in the wilderness is the only God that can provide security and fulfillment to their lives.

At this festival of remembrance, Jesus declared, "I am the light of the world" (John 8:12). Candelabras would have been aglow throughout the temple courtyards for the celebration, as Jesus declared, *"If you follow me, you won't have to walk in darkness, because you will have the light that leads to life"* (John 8:12).

The Pharisees couldn't find any defense to Jesus's claim except to say that He couldn't testify for Himself. They wanted witnesses to support this declaration. Jesus told them He could make this claim about Himself because He knew where He came from and where He was going. (See John 8:14.) Jesus knew He was God, but they didn't. God doesn't need a witness to prove who He is. Yet Jesus still gave them another witness, His Father in heaven.

John gives us specific details of Jesus's location when Christ professed to be the light of the world. *"Jesus made these statements while he was teaching in the section of the Temple known as the Treasury"* (John 8:20). This means Jesus was speaking in the Court of Women because the treasury was located there. The treasury consisted of thirteen contribution boxes used for collecting taxes and offerings. The boxes were narrow at the top and broad at the bottom, made to look like trumpets or shofars. Each contribution box was marked for a different type of offering.

The trumpet-shaped funnels guided the coins into the larger part of the container. Since they were made of bronze, the coins offered struck the metal and indicated how much people gave. People would often give for show rather than from the heart. In this backdrop of dark deceit, Jesus came to light the way.

Application:
As believers, we all have some places in our lives that are still prone to darkness. How can the light of Jesus reveal and dispel the dark areas of your life?

Prayer:
Jesus, shine Your light so that I won't walk in darkness. I want my motives and actions to reveal that You light the way in my life....

Day 27

SCRIPTURE READING: JOHN 8:31–47

Key Verses: John 8:31–38

Jesus said to the people who believed in him, "You are truly my disciples if you remain faithful to my teachings.

And you will know the truth, and the truth will set you free."

"But we are descendants of Abraham," they said. "We have never been slaves to anyone. What do you mean, 'You will be set free'?"

Jesus replied, "I tell you the truth, everyone who sins is a slave of sin. A slave is not a permanent member of the family, but a son is part of the family forever. So if the Son sets you free, you are truly free. Yes, I realize that you are descendants of Abraham. And yet some of you are trying to kill me because there's no room in your hearts for my message. I am telling you what I saw when I was with my Father. But you are following the advice of your father."

Explanation:

In our journey through John, we encounter yet another instance where religious leaders misunderstand Jesus. First, Jesus distinguished between true and false disciples by stating one guideline. True disciples faithfully obey God's Word. Next, Jesus connected obedience to knowing the truth. The way to know the truth is to live it! Jesus desired to show the religious leaders that when you genuinely experience the truth, that truth will set you free.

All the religious leaders heard from Jesus was the implication that they were not currently free. Sometimes, our narrow-mindedness causes us to be too easily offended, and we focus on what we think somebody is trying to say while missing the overall point of what they are saying. The only thing the Pharisees could think about was, "How dare Jesus think that we are slaves to anybody?" They referred to Abraham in their family tree and told Jesus, *"We have never been slaves to anyone"* (John 8:33).

The Pharisees couldn't stop thinking about the physical realm so Jesus could teach them about spiritual things. Too often, we get distracted by living in the natural world and miss the supernatural. Jesus was talking about spiritually being enslaved to sin, yet all they could fathom was someone questioning their physical freedom.

Jesus takes this discussion to another level when He starts talking about their father! They brought up Abraham and their family, so Jesus revealed who they really belonged to. Jesus's Father is God, while their father was the devil. This inflamed the religious leaders, who kept repeating, *"Our father is Abraham"* (John 8:39). Jesus goes straight to the lack of evidence to prove their claim. *"If you were really the children of Abraham, you would follow his example"* (John 8:39). Now, they knew Jesus was calling them illegitimate children, so they argued, *"God himself is our true Father"* (John 8:41). But Jesus replied, *"If God were your Father, you would love me, because I have come to you from God"* (John 8:42).

You can tell who your father is by your love and your actions. By their lack of love and legalistic lifestyle, the Pharisees showed who their real family was. They refused to listen to the truth of Jesus's teaching, and that is why they were never set free.

Application:

Sometimes, the truth hurts. But if we listen to the entirety of Jesus's teachings and follow Him, the truth can set us free.

Prayer:

God, I want to know and experience Your truth so that I can truly be set free. Help me to listen to You, even when the truth is hard to take....

Day 28

SCRIPTURE READING: JOHN 8:48–59

Key Verses: John 8:52–59

> The people said, "Now we know you are possessed by a demon. Even Abraham and the prophets died, but you say, 'Anyone who obeys my teaching will never die!' Are you greater than our father Abraham? He died, and so did the prophets. Who do you think you are?"
>
> Jesus answered, "If I want glory for myself, it doesn't count. But it is my Father who will glorify me. You say, 'He is our God,' but you don't even know him. I know him. If I said otherwise, I would be as great a liar as you! But I do know him and obey him. Your father Abraham rejoiced as he looked forward to my coming. He saw it and was glad."
>
> The people said, "You aren't even fifty years old. How can you say you have seen Abraham?"
>
> Jesus answered, "I tell you the truth, before Abraham was even born, I AM!" At that point they picked up stones to throw at him. But Jesus was hidden from them and left the Temple.

Scripture Reading: John 8:48–59 91

Explanation:

Yesterday, we read that Jesus told the Pharisees that God was not their father; the devil was. Now, I find it somewhat humorous that what follows in today's Scripture is the Pharisees claiming that Jesus is demon possessed. It reminds me of a small child when someone calls them a name, and they call them the same name right back. "No, I'm not, but you are." The Pharisees continue to show their lack of maturity and spiritual knowledge in every response they make to Jesus.

Here again, the religious leaders who studied for decades still needed to understand spiritual concepts. Jesus told them that whoever *"obeys my teaching will never die"* (John 8:52). Listen to their reasoning as they argue through comparison: *"Even Abraham and the prophets died....Are You greater than them?...Who do you think You are?"* (John 8:52–53). Didn't they realize from all their studies that the Messiah would come from God? Had it never occurred to them that if Jesus is who He says He is, He and His followers would live forever? They were so hung up on the religious tradition of Abraham that they failed to realize that Abraham believed in the same God that sent Jesus.

When we make idols out of our heritage, we miss the Savior who was sent from heaven. When we get stuck in the ruts of our religion, we will never reach the destination of a relationship with Christ. The Pharisees were so proud of their learning that they missed the teachings of the Lord.

While they continued to argue in their arrogance, the Pharisees missed the monumental truths of Jesus's message. They again went to the physical realm and contended, *"You aren't even fifty years old. How can you say you have* seen Abraham?" (John 8:57). Jesus answered them with this incredible truth, *"Before Abraham was even born, I AM!"* (John 8:58). They argued about age and father Abraham while speaking to the Son of God, who has always existed and was sent by the Father God.

Now, they are back to throwing stones. (See John 8:1–11.) They are so enraged that they pick up stones to kill Jesus. But God miraculously protects Christ by hiding Him from their sight. (See John 8:59.)

Application:
Some people would rather stay prideful and angry than admit they are wrong. How can you stay humble and teachable so that Jesus can teach you the great truths about Himself?

Prayer:
Lord, help me stay humble and teach me to listen....

Day 29

SCRIPTURE READING: JOHN 9:1–12

Key Verses: John 9:1–7

> As Jesus was walking along, he saw a man who had been blind from birth. "Rabbi," his disciples asked him, "why was this man born blind? Was it because of his own sins or his parents' sins?"
>
> "It was not because of his sins or his parents' sins," Jesus answered. "This happened so the power of God could be seen in him. We must quickly carry out the tasks assigned us by the one who sent us. The night is coming, and then no one can work. But while I am here in the world, I am the light of the world."
>
> Then he spit on the ground, made mud with the saliva, and spread the mud over the blind man's eyes. He told him, "Go wash yourself in the pool of Siloam" (Siloam means "sent"). So the man went and washed and came back seeing!

Explanation:

It wasn't just the Pharisees that misjudged Jesus. His disciples often misunderstood what Jesus said, too. We never arrive at the place where we know everything we need to know about Jesus. His attributes are unending, and His teachings continue to grow fruit in our lives as we faithfully follow Him. We must stay committed to following Jesus while we listen and learn.

Jesus and His disciples encountered a man who had been born blind. The disciples immediately misjudged this man's plight as punishment for somebody's sin. Jesus immediately corrects the false beliefs by stating, *"This happened so the power of God could be seen in him"* (John 9:3). God may allow us to encounter situations or suffer afflictions for His glory.

What Jesus says next seems on the surface to be out of place. (See John 9:4–5.) Why would Jesus tell His disciples here that they must quickly carry out God's work? Why would He infer that His stay on Earth was temporary? Why would He, the Light of the World, also say that night would come after He departed? Remember that everything Jesus says and when He says it are perfect. These statements from Jesus reveal God's perfect timing. This man's blindness and the fact that they met him on this day were all designed by God to coincide with this point in Jesus's earthly ministry. The man's physical darkness gave Jesus another opportunity to declare He was the Light of the World. The healing of the blind man demonstrated again God's power. Jesus's life on Earth would be short in light of eternity, so the disciples must work quickly and efficiently to learn everything they could while He was physically present with them.

The Lord Jesus lived with purpose every moment of His life, and He is teaching His disciples to do the same. Every moment we have is a gift from God and an opportunity to know Jesus better. If we live with this approach to life, we will see God in the details of each day.

Notice the detail even where Jesus sent the blind man to wash. Jesus said, *"Go wash in the pool of Siloam"* (John 9:7). God doesn't want us to miss the detail, so Scripture tells us that Siloam means "sent." The blind man was sent to a place that means sent. He went and came back seeing.

Application:

When we follow You, Lord, You will send us to specific places. When we obey and go where You send us, we will come back seeing more clearly spiritually!

Prayer:

Lord, help me see You more clearly by going where You send me. Help me see You in the details of every moment, knowing that You light the way....

Day 30

SCRIPTURE READING: JOHN 9:13–25

Key Verses: John 9:17–25

> Then the Pharisees again questioned the man who had been blind and demanded, "What's your opinion about this man who healed you?"
>
> The man replied, "I think he must be a prophet."
>
> The Jewish leaders still refused to believe the man had been blind and could now see, so they called in his parents. They asked them, "Is this your son? Was he born blind? If so, how can he now see?"
>
> His parents replied, "We know this is our son and that he was born blind, but we don't know how he can see or who healed him. Ask him. He is old enough to speak for himself." His parents said this because they were afraid of the Jewish leaders, who had announced that anyone saying Jesus was the Messiah would be expelled from the synagogue. That's why they said, "He is old enough. Ask him."
>
> So for the second time they called in the man who had been blind and told him, "God should get the glory for this, because we know this man Jesus is a sinner."

*"I don't know whether he is a sinner," the man replied.
"But I know this: I was blind, and now I can see!"*

Explanation:

Today, we continue the account of the man Jesus healed of blindness. The Pharisees were in a dilemma. They desperately needed to discredit Jesus's miracle, or many others would believe in Him. If this happened, they would lose credibility and standing before the people. The Pharisees knew that miracles were a sign from God (see John 3:2; 9:16), so they had to either cause others to doubt the miracle or believe in Jesus themselves. Since they could never get to the point of belief, they chose every way they could to reject the miracle.

They questioned the healed man on several occasions. Whenever they asked the man questions, he responded honestly about what he knew was true. Amazingly, the once-blind man seeks the truth, while those who studied the Scriptures searched for a way to blind others to the truth. These religious leaders even call in the blind man's parents and ask, *"Is this your son?"* (John 9:19). His parents verify that he is their son and that he was born blind while stating the truth that they don't know how he was healed. The harder they tried to cause people to doubt, the more reasons they gave them to believe!

The world continues to reject Jesus to this day. People who don't believe in Jesus will go to extreme measures to try to discredit the truth about Him. However, it is impossible to hide the overwhelming evidence that Jesus is the Savior of the world. The harder they try to doubt the truth, the more others can see their lies. Lies will eventually be revealed for what they are. Truth always prevails. The truth really will set you free. (See John 8:32.)

The Pharisees could not disprove the miracle, so they altered their tactic and attacked who Jesus was. They called Him a sinner. (See John 9:24.) People still use this tactic today. When you can't discredit the visible result, try to cast doubt on someone's character. The Pharisees could not hide the miracle and would have no chance of attacking the character of Jesus Christ.

The healed man exemplifies how to answer critics. *"I know this: I was blind, and now I can see!"* (John 9:25).

Application:
How does your life display the truth about the person of Jesus Christ?

Prayer:
May I lead people to the truth of who You are by simply testifying about what You have done in my life....

Day 31

SCRIPTURE READING: JOHN 9:26–41

Key Verses: John 9:35–41

> *When Jesus heard what had happened, he found the man and asked, "Do you believe in the Son of Man?"*
>
> *The man answered, "Who is he, sir? I want to believe in him."*
>
> *"You have seen him," Jesus said, "and he is speaking to you!"*
>
> *"Yes, Lord, I believe!" the man said. And he worshiped Jesus.*
>
> *Then Jesus told him, "I entered this world to render judgment—to give sight to the blind and to show those who think they see that they are blind."*
>
> *Some Pharisees who were standing nearby heard him and asked, "Are you saying we're blind?"*
>
> *"If you were blind, you wouldn't be guilty," Jesus replied. "But you remain guilty because you claim you can see."*

Explanation:

Jesus found the man He had just healed and rewarded him for his honesty. First, the Lord asked him the question we must all answer: *"Do you believe in the Son of Man?"* (John

9:35). The answer to that question determines where we will spend all eternity.

Notice that the man didn't give a typical church answer because he had no church background. If that question was asked to religious people, they would all say they believed, and that would end the conversation.

This man in John 9 answered with true honesty and sincerity. *"Who is he...? I want to believe in him"* (John 9:36). How refreshing to see someone who is willing to admit he doesn't know, but he wants to. So often, people either miss Jesus or delay their opportunity to know Him because of their pride and pretension. Don't allow pride or others' opinions to hinder your genuine relationship with Jesus Christ. Your salvation is way too important. Please don't ignore or casually glance at the question of who Jesus is.

This man in John 9 gets the greatest answer to this most crucial question. Jesus said, *"You have seen him,... and he is speaking to you"* (John 9:37). In today's terminology, Jesus said, "I am the One you have been looking for, and I am standing right here." Immediately, the man believed and worshipped Jesus. (See John 9:38.)

This man received double healing from Jesus. He was physically healed of his blindness, and God also opened his spiritual eyes to see the Son of Man. He received the most remarkable healing of all. He was forgiven of his sins, and his soul was saved the moment he placed his faith in Jesus.

In this powerful story, a blind man is healed and saved, and the Pharisees are considered guilty before God because they refuse to see. The man healed was born blind and received his sight. The Pharisees had everything they needed in the Scriptures to see who Jesus was, but they remained blind to who Christ was because of their unbelief.

Application:

Faith opens our spiritual eyes so that we can see that Jesus is the Son of God and the Savior of the world. How is your spiritual vision today?

Prayer:

Lord, open my eyes so that I can see You clearly. Break down my pride and any pretentious spirit in me. Please remove any blinders that I have that cause me to doubt, and strengthen my faith in You....

Day 32

SCRIPTURE READING: JOHN 10:1–21

Key Verses: John 10:7–13

> *I tell you the truth, I am the gate for the sheep. All who came before me were thieves and robbers. But the true sheep did not listen to them. Yes, I am the gate. Those who come in through me will be saved. They will come and go freely and will find good pastures. The thief's purpose is to steal and kill and destroy. My purpose is to give them a rich and satisfying life.*
>
> *I am the good shepherd. The good shepherd sacrifices his life for the sheep. A hired hand will run when he sees a wolf coming. He will abandon the sheep because they don't belong to him and he isn't their shepherd. And so the wolf attacks them and scatters the flock. The hired hand runs away because he's working only for the money and doesn't really care about the sheep.*

Explanation:

Jesus shares a great analogy of Himself as the Shepherd for His sheep. A shepherd has a tremendous responsibility to protect and provide for his sheep. The *Life Application Commentary: John* offers excellent insight into the shepherd's care of his sheep.

At night, the shepherd often would gather the sheep into a fold to protect them from thieves or wild animals. The sheepfolds were caves or open areas surrounded by walls made of stones or branches, eight to ten feet high. Sometimes, the top of the wall was lined with thorns to further discourage predators and thieves. The fold's single entrance made it easier for a shepherd to guard his flock. Often, several shepherds used a single fold and took turns guarding the entrance. In towns where many people each owned a few sheep, the combined herd was watched over by a shepherd. Mingling the animals was no problem since each flock responded readily to its shepherd's voice.

The *gate* (also translated as "door") is the main entrance. Jesus explained that anyone who tried to get in any other way besides going through the gate would be *a thief and a bandit* – that person would be up to no good.[6]

Amid this comparison of a shepherd to the Good Shepherd, Jesus shares His purpose for leaving heaven and coming to Earth. Jesus declared, *"The thief's purpose is to steal and kill and destroy. My purpose is to give them a rich and satisfying life"* (John 10:10).

The devil is the thief depicted in Jesus's analogy. The devil comes to do three things: steal, kill, and destroy. His purpose is to take everything from you. However, Jesus

---

6. Bruce B. Barton, Philip W. Comfort, David R. Veerman, Neil Wilson, *Life Application Bible Commentary: John*, ed. Grant Osborne and Philip W. Comfort (Tyndale House, 1993), 203–4.

comes to give you a rewarding life. Christ's ultimate purpose is to bring true fulfillment and joy.

The *New King James Version* translates John 10:10 as: *"The thief does not come except to steal, and to kill, and to destroy. I have come that they may have life, and that they may have it more abundantly."*

Application:

Look at the last statement of the *New King James Version* of John 10:10 and notice the comma. Then consider this question: Which side of the comma are you living on? Are you just living life and barely surviving, or are you experiencing the abundant life God has planned for you?

Prayer:

God, I want the more abundant life You have planned for me. Help me to trust You as the Good Shepherd to protect and provide for me....

Day 33

SCRIPTURE READING: JOHN 10:22–42

Key Verses: John 10:22–30

> It was now winter, and Jesus was in Jerusalem at the time of Hanukkah, the Festival of Dedication. He was in the Temple, walking through the section known as Solomon's Colonnade. The people surrounded him and asked, "How long are you going to keep us in suspense? If you are the Messiah, tell us plainly."
>
> Jesus replied, "I have already told you, and you don't believe me. The proof is the work I do in my Father's name.
>
> But you don't believe me because you are not my sheep. My sheep listen to my voice; I know them, and they follow me. I give them eternal life, and they will never perish. No one can snatch them away from me, for my Father has given them to me, and he is more powerful than anyone else. No one can snatch them from the Father's hand. The Father and I are one."

Explanation:

The Festival of Dedication, now called Hanukkah, occurred approximately two months after the Feast of Tabernacles. This feast occurs in December. This festival originated under Judas Maccabeus in 165 BC to commemorate the cleansing of the temple after Antiochus Epiphanes defiled it. So, this annual festival marked the rededication of the temple.

It seems somewhat redundant that John would say, *"It was now winter"* (John 10:22), because everyone would know when he said it was during Hanukah. Pastor Charles Swindoll states that John could have "been using the season to set the literary tone. The winter of Jesus' life was approaching."[7] Jesus is headed to the cross to surrender His life so that we could be forgiven of our sins. It was about to turn spiritually cold as the religious crowd would reject the Savior sent by God, the One the temple had been rededicated to in order to worship!

The people around Jesus asked Him, *"If you are the Messiah, tell us plainly"* (John 10:24). Jesus responded that He had already told them, but they would not believe. (See John 10:25.) Christ then explained that His evidence could be seen in His works. Through the signs He performed that were predicted by the Old Testament prophets, Jesus had given them more than enough proof of who He was. Then, Christ reverts to the shepherd-sheep analogy and bluntly tells them why they haven't believed: *"You don't believe me because you are not my sheep"* (John 10:26).

If Jesus is your Shepherd, you know His voice. If you are His sheep, the Good Shepherd knows you. When you are in the right relationship with Jesus Christ, you follow Him just like sheep follow their shepherd.

---

7. Charles R. Swindoll, *Swindoll's Living Insights on John: New Testament Commentary* (Tyndale House, 2014), 206.

Scripture records twenty-one times that Jesus told His disciples, *"Follow Me."* This declaration by Jesus means far more than simply answering His invitation. It implies much more than just walking behind Him and physically following His steps. Jesus tells His disciples to follow Him because He wants to transform their lives.

As His first disciples demonstrated, following Jesus requires giving up your old life, obeying His teachings, taking up your cross daily, and living out your commitment to Him.

Application:

In all honesty, answer these questions from your heart: Am I following Jesus or just fooling around? Do I know Him as the Good Shepherd, and does He know me?

Prayer:

Jesus, I want to know Your voice to follow Your will. Help me to take up my cross and follow You....

Day 34

SCRIPTURE READING: JOHN 11:1–16

Key Verses: John 11:1, 4–7, 11–15

A man named Lazarus was sick. He lived in Bethany with his sisters, Mary and Martha....

But when Jesus heard about it he said, "Lazarus's sickness will not end in death. No, it happened for the glory of God so that the Son of God will receive glory from this." So although Jesus loved Martha, Mary, and Lazarus, he stayed where he was for the next two days. Finally, he said to his disciples, "Let's go back to Judea."...

Then he said, "Our friend Lazarus has fallen asleep, but now I will go and wake him up."

The disciples said, "Lord, if he is sleeping, he will soon get better!" They thought Jesus meant Lazarus was simply sleeping, but Jesus meant Lazarus had died.

So he told them plainly, "Lazarus is dead. And for your sakes, I'm glad I wasn't there, for now you will really believe. Come, let's go see him."

Explanation:

John 11:1–16 deals with delays and death. When Jesus heard that Lazarus was sick, He waited until he died before He went to see him. This was an inexcusable delay if you were part of Lazarus's family. (See John 11:21.) If you were Lazarus, this was an intolerable delay. Can you think of a more difficult delay to deal with than death occurring while you wait for God to show up?

We can only imagine how Mary and Martha felt when their good friend and Savior, Jesus Christ, didn't arrive in time. Have you ever felt like God was late to your situation? Have you ever questioned God's timing?

Who likes to wait? If it is called "fast food," then we shouldn't have to wait for it, right? We are so impatient while driving that road rage is at an all-time high. If somebody doesn't hurry up and move to the fast lane, we will make a passing lane on the shoulder. We have all wanted to pray, "Lord, please give me patience, but hurry!"

However, today's Scripture teaches us that when we have to wait on God, we end up really believing in God. Our faith grows when we approach delays with confidence that God is still in control. However, our faith weakens when delays cause us to doubt God.

That is why, after Jesus told His disciples that Lazarus was dead, He said, *"And for your sakes, I'm glad I wasn't there, for now you will really believe"* (John 11:15). Jesus told them He was glad He wasn't there in time! What? And why? Because it would help His disciples *"really believe."*

Jesus knew what was in store for Lazarus and His disciples. Since we don't know our future, we should fully trust the One who knows everything. As we depend on Him daily, we must mature and trust His timing is best. In the waiting time, we have a choice to allow our faith to grow or our impatience to show. The waiting times reveal whether we really believe in God!

Application:

How do you typically deal with delays? How can you exercise your faith in the waiting times to grow to believe in God?

Prayer:

God, help me to trust You more during the waiting times. Please help my faith grow so that rather than doubting Your plans, I fully trust in Your purpose for this life You have blessed me with. Lord, help me to really believe in You when I'm facing delays....

Day 35

SCRIPTURE READING: JOHN 11:17–27

Key Verses: John 11:20–27

> *When Martha got word that Jesus was coming, she went to meet him. But Mary stayed in the house. Martha said to Jesus, "Lord, if only you had been here, my brother would not have died. But even now I know that God will give you whatever you ask."*
>
> *Jesus told her, "Your brother will rise again."*
>
> *"Yes," Martha said, "he will rise when everyone else rises, at the last day."*
>
> *Jesus told her, "I am the resurrection and the life. Anyone who believes in me will live, even after dying. Everyone who lives in me and believes in me will never ever die. Do you believe this, Martha?"*
>
> *"Yes, Lord," she told him. "I have always believed you are the Messiah, the Son of God, the one who has come into the world from God."*

Explanation:

When Jesus finally arrived in Bethany, Lazarus had been dead for four days. Lazarus's sisters heard that Jesus had finally come. Martha was the first to meet Jesus after their brother had died. The first words out of her mouth must have broken Jesus's heart: *"Lord, if only you had been here, my brother would not have died"* (John 11:21). However, she follows her statement of grief with an incredible statement of faith: *"But even now I know that God will give you whatever you ask"* (John 11:22).

How is your faith when you are faced with grief? Do you doubt God's goodness and power when you are confronted with the reality of death?

Martha had great faith but still had difficulty understanding Jesus's words. When Jesus used the word *"resurrection"* (verse 25), Martha's mind went directly to the resurrection of the dead during the end times. Jesus referred to Lazarus and the present time, while Martha's grief led her to focus on the distant future.

In answer to her confused state, Jesus makes one of the most remarkable statements about His identity found in all of Scripture. He said, *"I am the resurrection and the life. Anyone who believes in me will live, even after dying. Everyone who lives in me and believes in me will never ever die"* (John 11:25–26).

There are several incredible truths found in His statement. First, Jesus is the resurrection and the life. Wouldn't it suffice to say He is the resurrection? Doesn't resurrection imply life? However, Jesus is both resurrection and life. Not only does Jesus give us victory over death and provide us resurrection power, but He is also life. Jesus is the reason we live and the One who gives us our next breath. When Jesus is our life, we don't have to wait until death to experience His resurrection power.

Secondly, Jesus said that those who believe in Him will live after they die. He added that everyone who believes in Him will never die. Jesus is speaking about two lives: a physical one and a spiritual one. When believers physically breathe their last breath here on Earth, they will still live spiritually with Jesus forever. Therefore, our spiritual lives continue forever and never die.

Application:

After His unbelievable declaration, Jesus asked Martha, *"Do you believe this?"* (John 11:26). That is a question we must all answer. Do you believe that Jesus is the resurrection and the life? Do you believe that you will live after you die? Do you believe that your spiritual life never dies?

Prayer:

Lord, give me faith to trust what You say....

Day 36

SCRIPTURE READING: JOHN 11:28-44

Key Verses: John 11:38-44

> *Jesus was still angry as he arrived at the tomb, a cave with a stone rolled across its entrance. "Roll the stone aside," Jesus told them.*
>
> *But Martha, the dead man's sister, protested, "Lord, he has been dead for four days. The smell will be terrible."*
>
> *Jesus responded, "Didn't I tell you that you would see God's glory if you believe?" So they rolled the stone aside. Then Jesus looked up to heaven and said, "Father, thank you for hearing me. You always hear me, but I said it out loud for the sake of all these people standing here, so that they will believe you sent me." Then Jesus shouted, "Lazarus, come out!" And the dead man came out, his hands and feet bound in graveclothes, his face wrapped in a headcloth. Jesus told them, "Unwrap him and let him go!"*

Explanation:

Jesus was angry when He arrived at the tomb of Lazarus. The word *"angry"* comes from a New Testament word, *embrimaomai*, which means "to be moved with anger and to express strong indignation."[8] The Greek root word, *brimaomai*, literally means "to snort." It would be similar to an angry horse snorting with anger and roaring with rage. What was Jesus so mad about when He reached Lazarus's grave?

To answer that question, one can only speculate. Nevertheless, as we ponder His emotions, we must remember that Scripture clearly states that Jesus was sinless (see 2 Corinthians 5:21, 1 Peter 2:22, Hebrews 4:15.) We also know that Paul wrote, *"In your anger do not sin"* (Ephesians 4:26 NIV). Since Jesus never sinned, and it is possible to be angry and not sin, what angered Jesus?

Several scholars agree that it is highly likely that Jesus was angered at death and the sorrow and separation that it brings. Since Jesus is life, it is logical to say that He hates death and what it causes. According to John 11:35, Jesus loved this family so much that He wept over their suffering. Therefore, it is safe to say that Jesus grieves over the grief death brings.

Jesus came to conquer sin, death, hell, and the grave. His death on the cross would bring victory over sin and hell, while His resurrection would triumph over death and the grave. Jesus lived a sinless life so that He could die a sacrificial death so that you and I could be saved from our sins and experience the power of His resurrection.

When Jesus called Lazarus from the grave, He illustrated His resurrection power for all humanity. At first, Lazarus came from his tomb bound in grave clothes. Then, Jesus ordered that the death wrappings be removed so that

---

8. "1690. Embrimaomai," *BibleHub*, accessed March 5, 2025, https://biblehub.com/greek/1690.htm.

he could be truly set free. I love how the *New King James Version* translates Jesus's words in John 11:44: *"Loose him, and let him go."*

Jesus came to remove the power death held over every sinner. Paul summed up Jesus's conquest: *"For the wages of sin is death, but the free gift of God is eternal life through Christ Jesus our Lord"* (Romans 6:23).

Application:

Have you been set free from the penalty and power of death through the free gift of eternal life by accepting Jesus Christ as Savior and Lord? Have you been set free regarding the grave wrappings of your old life?

Prayer:

Thank You, Lord, thank You for showing Your power over death through Lazarus, even before demonstrating it again at Your empty tomb. Please help me to live free from anything that slightly resembles the wrappings of the old life....

Day 37

SCRIPTURE READING: JOHN 11:45–57

Key Verses: John 11:45–52

> Many of the people who were with Mary believed in Jesus when they saw this happen. But some went to the Pharisees and told them what Jesus had done. Then the leading priests and Pharisees called the high council together. "What are we going to do?" they asked each other. "This man certainly performs many miraculous signs. If we allow him to go on like this, soon everyone will believe in him. Then the Roman army will come and destroy both our Temple and our nation."
>
> Caiaphas, who was high priest at that time, said, "You don't know what you're talking about! You don't realize that it's better for you that one man should die for the people than for the whole nation to be destroyed."
>
> He did not say this on his own; as high priest at that time he was led to prophesy that Jesus would die for the entire nation. And not only for that nation, but to bring together and unite all the children of God scattered around the world.

Explanation:

Everyone, at some time in their earthly life, must answer, "What will I do with Jesus?" Jesus had brought Lazarus back to life. Each witness to Jesus's resurrection miracle was faced with a choice: "Will I believe in Jesus, or will I reject Him?"

As we read the conclusion to the story, it is not surprising to find that there were people left in two opposing groups: one group put their trust in Jesus, and the other failed to believe. John 11:45 reveals that some people who had come with Mary to Lazarus's tomb *"believed in Jesus."* However, no sooner than John records those who believed, we are confronted with those who disbelieved. The leading priests and Pharisees called the high council to discuss what to do so they could stop everyone from believing in Jesus. Isn't it ironic that the religious people, who thought they were good, rejected Jesus while those who recognized they weren't good and were sinners received Jesus by faith? These religious rulers did something worse than disbelieving; they blatantly sought to kill Jesus and His testimony.

God speaks a prophetic word through Caiaphas, the High Priest, who says to the council, *"You don't realize that it's better for you that one man should die for the people than for the whole nation to be destroyed"* (John 11:50). Here is what Caiaphas meant by quoting a proverbial statement of his day and time: "It is better that Jesus be killed, than if He is left alone and He stirs up the anger of Rome against all the Jewish people." In other words, an innocent Messiah should die before a massacre takes place. However, God allowed this statement to speak prophetic to mean that Jesus would die for the sins of the world so that we wouldn't have to die for our sins.

God is in control. He can take the words of those who don't believe in Him and use them to declare His good news to the world. Just like in Jesus's day, there will always be two groups: those who believe in Jesus and those who reject Him. The same evidence is available to all people. Which group will you be in?

Application:

"What will you do with Jesus?"

Prayer:

Lord, I want to believe in You. In light of all the evidence, please help me to trust You more. Strengthen my faith and dispel my doubts so that I can live with complete confidence and assurance that You are the Savior who died for the whole world....

Day 38

SCRIPTURE READING: JOHN 12:1–19

Key Verses: John 12:1–8

> Six days before the Passover celebration began, Jesus arrived in Bethany, the home of Lazarus—the man he had raised from the dead. A dinner was prepared in Jesus' honor. Martha served, and Lazarus was among those who ate with him. Then Mary took a twelve-ounce jar of expensive perfume made from essence of nard, and she anointed Jesus' feet with it, wiping his feet with her hair. The house was filled with the fragrance.
>
> But Judas Iscariot, the disciple who would soon betray him, said, "That perfume was worth a year's wages. It should have been sold and the money given to the poor." Not that he cared for the poor—he was a thief, and since he was in charge of the disciples' money, he often stole some for himself.
>
> Jesus replied, "Leave her alone. She did this in preparation for my burial. You will always have the poor among you, but you will not always have me."

Explanation:

Jesus's visit to Lazarus's house reveals three types of people usually found in God's house, the church. The first type, depicted by Martha, is a serving church member. Scripture tells us that Martha served. They were preparing a meal to honor Jesus. Martha was serving Jesus and those around her by helping with the meal. We honor Jesus by the way we serve.

The New Testament word for "serve" in John 12:2 is *diakoneó*, from which the word "deacon" is derived. It is defined as "to serve" or "to minister." It means "kicking up dust because you are on the move."[9] In the dusty streets and houses of Bethany, Martha was on the move, stirring up dust as she ministered to others.

The second type of person, represented by Mary, is the worshipping church member. While Martha concentrated on serving Jesus, Mary focused on praising Him. John tells us that Mary took a twelve-ounce jar filled with a perfume called essence of nard and anointed Jesus's feet. Judas tells us in verse 5 that this sacrifice of praise was valued at a year's wages. Mary demonstrated her love for Jesus by pouring out her praise to the Lord. Scripture tells us that *"the house was filled with the fragrance"* (John 12:3). True worship is a pleasing aroma to the Lord and impacts those in God's house.

The third type of church member is illustrated through Judas. This is the selfish church member who cares about nothing but himself. While Mary poured out her praise, Judas poured on his criticism. Rather than think about Jesus being worthy of worship, all he could focus on was how much the perfume was worth. Scripture tells us explicitly that not only was he in charge of the disciples' money, but he also stole from them. (See John 12:6.)

---

9. "1247. Diakoneó," *BibleHub*, accessed March 5, 2025, https://biblehub.com/greek/1247.htm.

Therefore, we see three types of church members at Lazarus's house: one served, one worshipped, and the other was a selfish thief. Remember that Jesus knows why we come to church and exactly which type of church member we are. Jesus stands up for those who served and worshipped Him, while He stands against those with selfish motives.

Application:

Which type of church member best described your attitude and actions?

Prayer:

Jesus, please give me a passion to worship You no matter the cost. Help me to love You so much that I kick up some dust in ministering to others, knowing that in doing so, I am also serving and honoring You....

Day 39

SCRIPTURE READING: JOHN 12:20–36

Key Verses: John 12:20–26

> *Some Greeks who had come to Jerusalem for the Passover celebration paid a visit to Philip, who was from Bethsaida in Galilee. They said, "Sir, we want to meet Jesus." Philip told Andrew about it, and they went together to ask Jesus.*
>
> *Jesus replied, "Now the time has come for the Son of Man to enter into his glory. I tell you the truth, unless a kernel of wheat is planted in the soil and dies, it remains alone. But its death will produce many new kernels—a plentiful harvest of new lives. Those who love their life in this world will lose it. Those who care nothing for their life in this world will keep it for eternity. Anyone who wants to serve me must follow me, because my servants must be where I am. And the Father will honor anyone who serves me."*

Explanation:

Have you ever sent your children to accomplish a task and then returned only to find they hadn't even attempted to do what you told them to do? I remember my parents having that same problem with me. My parents would tell me exactly what had to be done and when—by the time they got home. I remember seeing my dad's car pull into our driveway and panicking because I had not done what he told me to do. It never pleased my father when I disobeyed.

Scripture makes it clear that saved people follow God and serve Him. As exemplified in a kernel of wheat dying to produce a harvest, God has called us to die to ourselves so we can live for Him. If we aren't willing to die to our daily desires, we will never find the joy of the harvest. Our God specializes in bringing dead things to life. The power of the resurrection flows through surrendered lives.

We can't wait to see our Heavenly Father returning to do what He has called us to do. Delayed obedience is still disobedience. John 12:25 defines our dilemma. We lose our way when we love our life more than we love our Lord. We must die daily to our selfish desires if we are going to live for Jesus Christ.

Perhaps we have let our comfortable Christianity cause us to miss the call of Christ. An outward religion will never give us enough motivation to live out God's calling for our lives. However, when we fall in love with our Lord, we will long for a close relationship with Him. When you love someone, you care about what they care about. Their passions become your passions. Those who truly follow Jesus find their fulfillment through their relationship with Him. Serving God is no longer something you do because you feel guilty when you don't. Serving God becomes something you are excited about and enjoy because you love Him. When you move past a religion and find a relationship with God, you discover the difference between doing things for God and spending life with God.

Application:

In what areas of your life are you living for yourself rather than for God?

Prayer:

Lord, help me to die to my worldly desires so I can follow Your will. Please give me a genuine desire to follow You and serve You because I love You more than anything....

Day 40

SCRIPTURE READING: JOHN 12:37–50

Key Verses: John 12:37, 42–50

> But despite all the miraculous signs Jesus had done, most of the people still did not believe in him.
>
> Many people did believe in him, however, including some of the Jewish leaders. But they wouldn't admit it for fear that the Pharisees would expel them from the synagogue. For they loved human praise more than the praise of God.
>
> Jesus shouted to the crowds, "If you trust me, you are trusting not only me, but also God who sent me. For when you see me, you are seeing the one who sent me. I have come as a light to shine in this dark world, so that all who put their trust in me will no longer remain in the dark. I will not judge those who hear me but don't obey me, for I have come to save the world and not to judge it. But all who reject me and my message will be judged on the day of judgment by the truth I have spoken. I don't speak on my own authority. The Father who sent me has commanded me what to say and how to say it. And I know his commands lead to eternal life; so I say whatever the Father tells me to say."

Explanation:

Jesus has entered His final week before the cross, and His public ministry is coming to a close. After three years of ministering, teaching, and proving Himself through incredible miracles, *"most of the people still did not believe in him"* (John 12:37). John reminded his readers in John 12:38–41 that God had prophesied some seven hundred years earlier through the prophet Isaiah about this unbelief. (See Isaiah 53:1, 6:10.) Isaiah 53 foretells not only that these people will disbelieve, but that they also will despise and reject Jesus. Christ had given them every reason imaginable to believe, but in their stubborn hearts, they still chose to reject Him.

However, John shares that many people still believed in Him, including some of the Jewish leaders. When Jesus's earthly ministry began, the Jewish leaders hated Him the most. Now, we discover that some who first doubted and disbelieved eventually put their trust in Jesus Christ. This good news is immediately followed by bad news. Even though they finally believed, they still weren't willing to risk losing their status and position at the synagogue. They were so concerned with losing their popularity that they wouldn't publicly admit that they believed in Jesus.

In Matthew 10:32–33, Jesus plainly said:

Everyone who acknowledges me publicly here on earth, I will also acknowledge before my Father in heaven. But everyone who denies me here on earth, I will also deny before my Father in heaven.

It will be a tragic day for those Jesus denies before His Father. If we refuse to confess Jesus as Lord here, we cannot do so in heaven. John tells us why these people who thought

Jesus was the Messiah would never surrender their lives to Him: *"For they loved human praise more than the praise of God"* (John 12:43). The bottom line is that these people loved themselves more than they loved Jesus.

Application:

Jesus is not looking for secret or silent believers. How are you publicly living for Christ?

Prayer:

God, one day, I want You to confess me before Your Father in heaven. Please give me the courage to confess You to those around me today. Help me to love You more than anything or anyone else—including myself....

Day 41

SCRIPTURE READING: JOHN 13:1–20

Key Verses: John 13:1–5, 12–15

Before the Passover celebration, Jesus knew that his hour had come to leave this world and return to his Father. He had loved his disciples during his ministry on earth, and now he loved them to the very end. It was time for supper, and the devil had already prompted Judas, son of Simon Iscariot, to betray Jesus. Jesus knew that the Father had given him authority over everything and that he had come from God and would return to God. So he got up from the table, took off his robe, wrapped a towel around his waist, and poured water into a basin. Then he began to wash the disciples' feet, drying them with the towel he had around him....

After washing their feet, he put on his robe again and sat down and asked, "Do you understand what I was doing? You call me 'Teacher' and 'Lord,' and you are right, because that's what I am. And since I, your Lord and Teacher, have washed your feet, you ought to wash each other's feet. I have given you an example to follow. Do as I have done to you."

Explanation:

John 13 begins what many call Jesus's upper room discourse. John records this intimate conversation between Jesus and His disciples in chapters 13–17. This section of Jesus's teaching only occurs in the Gospel of John, beginning with Jesus washing His disciples' feet.

In biblical times, the roads were not paved, and those who could afford shoes had only one option—open-toed sandals. This led to some dirty feet! So when you went to visit someone at their home, the host would have a servant meet you outside the door of their home with a basin of water and a towel. You would remove your shoes if you owned a pair, and the servant would kneel and wash your dirty feet.

With that background, let's look at Jesus's incredible example of a servant found in John 13. Jesus knew the cross was before Him, so He got up from the table and washed the disciples' feet. The Lord of all knelt before all of His disciples. Our Savior not only took on the nature of a servant when He left His throne room in Glory (see Philippians 2:7), but He knelt to serve His followers just days before His final sacrifice at Calvary. It is important to note that before He hung on the cross, He picked up a towel and washed His disciples' feet.

When Jesus got to Simon Peter to wash his feet, Peter objected. *"'You will never ever wash my feet!' Jesus replied, 'Unless I wash you, you won't belong to me'"* (John 13:8). Impetuous Peter jumped to the other extreme and said, *"Then wash my hands and head as well"* (John 13:9). Jesus gave this profound reply: *"A person who has bathed all over does not need to wash, except for the feet, to be entirely clean*" (John 13:10).

Jesus used the washing of feet to symbolize our daily need for forgiveness and the taking of a bath to denote our salvation. By washing His disciples' feet, Jesus gave them an example of service to follow and taught them to apply cleansing to their daily lives. Salvation is a one-time cleansing experience that leads to an ongoing daily walk of purity. People with clean lives know how important it is to serve others and Jesus Christ.

Application:

Just as dirt was on their feet, sin is in our lives. Have you been washed clean by being saved, and are you picking up the towel to serve?

Prayer:

Lord, wash me clean of the sin in my life. Please help me to serve others with the attitude that no task is beneath me. May I follow the example You set for serving....

Day 42

SCRIPTURE READING: JOHN 13:21–30

Key Verses: John 13:21–30

Now Jesus was deeply troubled, and he exclaimed, "I tell you the truth, one of you will betray me!"

The disciples looked at each other, wondering whom he could mean. The disciple Jesus loved was sitting next to Jesus at the table. Simon Peter motioned to him to ask, "Who's he talking about?" So that disciple leaned over to Jesus and asked, "Lord, who is it?"

Jesus responded, "It is the one to whom I give the bread I dip in the bowl." And when he had dipped it, he gave it to Judas, son of Simon Iscariot. When Judas had eaten the bread, Satan entered into him. Then Jesus told him, "Hurry and do what you're going to do." None of the others at the table knew what Jesus meant. Since Judas was their treasurer, some thought Jesus was telling him to go and pay for the food or to give some money to the poor. So Judas left at once, going out into the night.

Explanation:

Jesus had just washed all the disciples' feet, including Judas. Knowing that Judas would betray Him didn't change the demonstration of Jesus's love toward His betrayer. God's love is unconditional. God doesn't love you because you deserve it; He loves you because He is the God of love. God loves you because of who He is, not who you are. His nature will not allow Him to stop loving you because His love is unending, underserved, and unconditional.

The Bread of Life dipped a piece of bread into a dish and handed it to the one who would betray Him for thirty pieces of silver. (See Matthew 26:15). In Exodus 21:32, we are told that thirty pieces of silver was the price of a servant. Jesus humbled Himself as a servant, washing His disciples' feet—even those of Judas—and was betrayed for the price of a servant.

Jesus, the King of Kings and Lord of Lords, was also a humble servant who submitted to the will of His Father. God's will included allowing Jesus to be betrayed and crucified because God's love is limitless.

John 13:30 could serve a dual purpose. It reads, "*So Judas left at once, going out into the night.*" The time tells us a sad story. "Night" tells us what time of day it was, but it also describes the spiritual state of Judas's soul. It was dark outside, but it was also spiritually dark in Judas's heart. While the Son of God was unconditionally loving Judas, this betrayer had no light in his heart toward God.

In a world filled with spiritual darkness, remember that Jesus is the Light of the World. (See John 8:12.) In the presence of the Son, we should never see spiritual darkness. The choice is ours: to follow the light of day or live in the darkness of night. Judas made the wrong choice and suffered the eternal fate of betraying Jesus.

Jesus will love you unconditionally because that is His nature, but don't forget that He is also a righteous judge. The same God who loves the sinner still has to judge our sins. That is why He sent His Son Jesus to die in our place. If you receive the light of Jesus by faith, your sins are paid for at the cross. If you reject Jesus and His sacrifice, you will be judged for your sins. Don't betray the unconditional love of Jesus by refusing to receive the gift of salvation and all He has done to forgive your sins.

Application:
Like Judas, how do people betray Jesus today?

Prayer:
Lord, thank You for loving me unconditionally, offering me the gift of salvation through Your sacrifice, and giving me free will to decide. May I never betray Your love for me....

Day 43

SCRIPTURE READING: JOHN 13:31–38

Key Verses: John 13:31–38

> As soon as Judas left the room, Jesus said, "The time has come for the Son of Man to enter into his glory, and God will be glorified because of him. And since God receives glory because of the Son, he will give his own glory to the Son, and he will do so at once. Dear children, I will be with you only a little longer. And as I told the Jewish leaders, you will search for me, but you can't come where I am going. So now I am giving you a new commandment: Love each other. Just as I have loved you, you should love each other. Your love for one another will prove to the world that you are my disciples."
>
> Simon Peter asked, "Lord, where are you going?"
>
> And Jesus replied, "You can't go with me now, but you will follow me later."
>
> "But why can't I come now, Lord?" he asked. "I'm ready to die for you."
>
> Jesus answered, "Die for me? I tell you the truth, Peter—before the rooster crows tomorrow morning, you will deny three times that you even know me."

Explanation:

Jesus had just foretold that Judas would betray Him. Now, He tells Peter that he will deny Him. The Son of God was betrayed and denied by two people who followed Him for three years. Let that statement sink into your hearts for a few minutes.

Like Peter, we are often unfaithful to God. However, God is always faithful to us. This is precisely what Paul wrote to Timothy in 2 Timothy 2:13: *"If we are unfaithful, he remains faithful, for he cannot deny who he is."*

I have known several people who stopped following God because someone who claimed to be a Christian hurt and betrayed them. The unfaithfulness and animosity of others will never diminish God's faithfulness and love. While we should never be a spiritual stumbling block to others, God's character is never changed by the actions of sinners. God is the same yesterday, today, and forever. (See Hebrews 13:8.)

Peter denied Jesus, and Judas betrayed Him. Out of His love, He offered forgiveness to both of them. Peter accepted God's love and would later be restored. In contrast, Judas ends his life before he ever embraces God's love.

What caused Judas's betrayal and Peter's denial? Judas betrayed Jesus because he expected a Messiah who would rule over the Romans, not surrender and die for the sins of the world. Judas missed Jesus because of his preconceived ideas and false beliefs.

On the other hand, Peter denied Jesus because he felt he had been left alone. He couldn't understand that Jesus would prepare a place for him in heaven and one day return to call all His children home. He thought Jesus was going away for good and didn't realize He would leave the Holy Spirit to protect, provide, and guide him. Thus, Peter denied Jesus because He misunderstood God's plan.

Application:

Don't let your wrong ideas about Jesus or your misguided thoughts about His will for your life cause you to deny or betray Him. When you fail, be quick to turn back to God and receive His love and forgiveness.

Prayer:

Help me to trust You and Your will for my life. Don't let my false assumptions or misunderstanding keep me from a relationship with You....

Day 44

SCRIPTURE READING: JOHN 14:1–14

Key Verses: John 14:1–6

> "Don't let your hearts be troubled. Trust in God, and trust also in me. There is more than enough room in my Father's home. If this were not so, would I have told you that I am going to prepare a place for you? When everything is ready, I will come and get you, so that you will always be with me where I am. And you know the way to where I am going."
>
> "No, we don't know, Lord," Thomas said. "We have no idea where you are going, so how can we know the way?"
>
> Jesus told him, "I am the way, the truth, and the life. No one can come to the Father except through me."

Explanation:

Jesus's first disciples faced the fears of an unknown future. They were disturbed deep in their souls. They had just learned that Judas would betray Jesus and that Peter would deny Him. They were likely questioning their loyalty to Jesus and scared about the growing opposition surrounding Him from the religious crowd.

Where do you turn first when you are stressed out and overcome with anxiety? What do you do when your heart is troubled?

Jesus, knowing their struggle, shares some great news with His followers. When you listen to His words in John 14, Jesus can bring help for your troubled heart. Jesus began with these words: *"Don't let your hearts be troubled"* (John 14:1). The word Christ used for "troubled" is intriguing in Greek. The word is only found eighteen times in the New Testament. It is the word *tarassó*, which means "emotional agitation from getting too stirred up inside."[10] This word can also mean "to set in motion what needs to remain still."[11] Sometimes, trouble can shake us up and make us feel like our hearts have been thrown into the spin cycle of a washing machine. However, when trouble surrounds you, your heart must stay calm and at ease.

Jesus says to trust in Him when circumstances shake up your emotions. When your feelings are stirred up and mixed up, place all your faith in God your Father. When this world doesn't make sense, place all your trust in the One who created it all.

In the original language, the second sentence in John 14:1 is inverted and reads, "Trust in God, in Me also trust." When you read Jesus's words in that order, trust becomes the two bookends of His statement, while Jesus becomes the center of your focus. Putting God in the center of our hearts, surrounded by our trust in Him, can bring rest to our agitated lives.

---

10. "5015. Tarassó," BibleHub, accessed March 6, 2025, https://biblehub.com/greek/5015.htm.
11. BibleHub, "5015. Tarassó."

Jesus then told them that He would prepare a place for them and return and take them there. (See John 14:2.) In sincere doubt, Thomas said, "*We have no idea where you are going, so how can we know the way?*" (John 14:5). Jesus's response is one of the most extraordinary statements found in Scripture. "*I am the way, the truth, and the life. No one can come to the Father except through me*" (John 14:6). Jesus is the way; it is only through Jesus that believers have a path to reach God. Jesus is the truth; His teachings are the only reliable source of divine wisdom. Jesus is the life; our only true satisfaction comes through a relationship with Him.

Application:

How can you keep Jesus at the center of your life, surrounded by your trust in Him?

Prayer:

I pray today that I will trust in You, Jesus, so that my heart won't be troubled....

Day 45

SCRIPTURE READING: JOHN 14:15–31

Key Verses: John 14:15–21

> "If you love me, obey my commandments. And I will ask the Father, and he will give you another Advocate, who will never leave you. He is the Holy Spirit, who leads into all truth. The world cannot receive him, because it isn't looking for him and doesn't recognize him. But you know him, because he lives with you now and later will be in you. No, I will not abandon you as orphans—I will come to you. Soon the world will no longer see me, but you will see me. Since I live, you also will live. When I am raised to life again, you will know that I am in my Father, and you are in me, and I am in you. Those who accept my commandments and obey them are the ones who love me. And because they love me, my Father will love them. And I will love them and reveal myself to each of them."

Explanation:

Many who reject Jesus say that Christianity is just a legalistic set of rules. The world implies that following Jesus is not any fun because of all the things God doesn't allow you to do. It becomes even more troubling when individuals identifying as Christians concentrate solely on what God prohibits, neglecting the many blessings that Jesus offers in our lives. True believers can even have the mindset of enduring their Christian life instead of enjoying all the benefits of knowing Jesus Christ.

When Jesus said, *"If you love me, obey my commandments"* (John 14:15), that was not legalism. It was love! God gave us commandments to obey because He loves us and wants to protect us.

Any good father gives his children strong commands to protect them from the consequences of bad decisions. What father wouldn't warn his children about the dangers of playing with fire? What kind of father wouldn't demand his children stay away from strangers? Our God is a perfect heavenly Father, so He must give commandments to His children so they don't miss His best for their lives.

As a child, I didn't understand my father's rules. As a teenager, I often questioned him and his rules. However, when I matured, I understood that the rules were there because my father loved me. When I became a father myself, I fully comprehended the weight of responsibility fathers carry for their children's safety and well-being.

Likewise, the more we grow in our Christian walk, the more we realize that His commandments are there because Christ loves us. When we realize how much He loves us, we obey His commands because we love Him, too. It is out of a loving relationship that we desire to obey God, knowing that rules are made from His love. I once heard a pastor say that a Christian's obedience towards Father God is not a have-to obedience but a want-to obedience. That is because both sides of the relationship are motivated by love!

Application:

Have you reached a point in your journey with God where you view His commands as displays of His love for you? How does true joy come through a relationship with Jesus motivated by love?

Prayer:

Father God, thank You for loving me so much that You set rules to protect me. Help me see Your laws as displays of Your love. May I also realize that it is my obedience that reveals my true love back to You....

Day 46

SCRIPTURE READING: JOHN 15:1–17

Key Verses: John 15:1, 4–8

> *I am the true grapevine, and my Father is the gardener....*
>
> *Remain in me, and I will remain in you. For a branch cannot produce fruit if it is severed from the vine, and you cannot be fruitful unless you remain in me.*
>
> *Yes, I am the vine; you are the branches. Those who remain in me, and I in them, will produce much fruit. For apart from me you can do nothing. Anyone who does not remain in me is thrown away like a useless branch and withers. Such branches are gathered into a pile to be burned. But if you remain in me and my words remain in you, you may ask for anything you want, and it will be granted! When you produce much fruit, you are my true disciples. This brings great glory to my Father.*

Explanation:

The essence of Christianity is a relationship with Jesus Christ that involves abiding in Him. We must stay connected to Jesus to receive His life-giving sustenance. This can only take place with consistent communication with

Christ. Therefore, an abiding relationship with Jesus is only possible through a lifestyle of prayer.

Martin Luther King, Jr., once said, "To be a Christian without prayer is no more possible than to be alive without breathing."[12] This is the truth that Jesus refers to as He discusses with His disciples that He is the vine. We are merely branches that have one responsibility: remain in Christ. In other words, stay connected so that we will produce fruit.

The importance of connection is displayed in many areas of our lives. For example, if we don't connect our cell phones to a charger, they will eventually die. All the capability of technology in the world is of no value unless it is connected to a power source. The endless power of our omnipotent God will not flow through our lives if we are detached from Him.

If you have ever bought a ticket to a sporting event, you will notice the perforated section on one side with these words: "Not good if detached." If you tear off the side for entry before you arrive, you will not be allowed into the game. The same concept is true in our spiritual lives. God will not allow us into the eternal event if we are not attached through a real relationship with Christ. Communication and connection are vital parts of our everyday lives.

If you only pray occasionally, you will have a sporadic relationship with Jesus. You can't expect to pray meaningless words to Him and have a meaningful relationship with Him. Neither can you pray once a week and still have a strong walk with your Lord. It will take a dedicated lifestyle of prayer to have a life devoted to your Lord. It will take

---

12. Charles R. Swindoll, *The Tale of the Tardy Oxcart and 1,501 Other Stories* (Thomas Nelson, 2016), 450.

a desperate and dependent approach to God to find Him fully.

Application:

How is your connection with Christ? In what ways does your communication with Jesus need improvement?

Prayer:

Lord, it is vitally important that I stay connected to You. Please keep me constantly connected to You through a strong prayer life....

Day 47

SCRIPTURE: JOHN 15:18–27

Key Verses: John 15:20–27

> Do you remember what I told you? "A slave is not greater than the master." Since they persecuted me, naturally they will persecute you. And if they had listened to me, they would listen to you. They will do all this to you because of me, for they have rejected the one who sent me. They would not be guilty if I had not come and spoken to them. But now they have no excuse for their sin. Anyone who hates me also hates my Father. If I hadn't done such miraculous signs among them that no one else could do, they would not be guilty. But as it is, they have seen everything I did, yet they still hate me and my Father. This fulfills what is written in their Scriptures: "They hated me without cause."
>
> But I will send you the Advocate—the Spirit of truth. He will come to you from the Father and will testify all about me. And you must also testify about me because you have been with me from the beginning of my ministry.

Explanation:

Today, there is a considerable increase in "prosperity gospel" teaching. These false teachings claim that by following Jesus, you will prosper with better health, riches, and accomplishments. Sometimes, preachers can be blunt about God promising to bless you; others are more subtle in their approach. Whichever the case, the "prosperity gospel" teachings are misleading to many believers.

What happens when you follow Jesus, and you don't become more wealthy, powerful, or successful by the world's definition? Do you begin to doubt God because you didn't receive what teachers promised? Do you suspect that maybe something is wrong with you because you aren't as successful as you thought you would be? The answer is no on both questions. It wasn't God's fault, nor yours. It was the fact that you believed in false teachings.

Jesus never taught that following Him would be easy or financially beneficial. In today's Scripture, Jesus taught His first disciples a different message. Jesus plainly told them that they would be persecuted.

He argued that a slave is not better than his master. The world will not treat the followers of Christ better than it treated Jesus. The world hated Jesus, and the world will hate those who fully commit themselves to following Jesus Christ.

The darkness is always in direct conflict with the light. Light exposes the darkness. Nobody likes to have their sins exposed. You likely didn't like it the first time you were convicted of your sins. Most of us fought against God's calling on our lives because we didn't want to admit to anyone, much less ourselves, that we were sinners. It takes time to surrender your heart to the truth of who you are. It requires brutal honesty with yourself to admit that you need God. It is natural for your flesh to fight against what God seeks to do in your spirit.

The world, full of fleshy desires and unyielded hearts, will attack those who suggest they need help and have sins that must be forgiven. Just as they treated Jesus, the world will hate both the message and the messenger.

Just know that when you are persecuted for following God's will, you are in good company, the same company as your Savior, Jesus Christ!

Application:

How are you tempted to doubt God or yourself when you don't receive some worldly benefits?

Prayer:

Jesus, please give me the strength to follow You no matter what comes my way in this fallen world....

Day 48

SCRIPTURE READING: JOHN 16:1–15

Key Verses: John 16:1–8

> I have told you these things so that you won't abandon your faith. For you will be expelled from the synagogues, and the time is coming when those who kill you will think they are doing a holy service for God. This is because they have never known the Father or me. Yes, I'm telling you these things now, so that when they happen, you will remember my warning. I didn't tell you earlier because I was going to be with you for a while longer.
>
> But now I am going away to the one who sent me, and not one of you is asking where I am going. Instead, you grieve because of what I've told you. But in fact, it is best for you that I go away, because if I don't, the Advocate won't come. If I do go away, then I will send him to you. And when he comes, he will convict the world of its sin, and of God's righteousness, and of the coming judgment.

Explanation:

Jesus told His disciples they would face hardships because of following Him. He warned them before these difficult times occurred so they would not abandon their faith. The word for "abandon, stumble, or fall away" (depending on your translation) is the Greek word *skandalizó*. This is where we get our English word "scandal." The word can mean "to set as a snare, to hinder right conduct or thought, or to cause to stumble."[13] Jesus cautioned His first followers not to let hard times cause them to fall into the trap of questioning their faith. When tough times come, and they will, don't let it hinder how you think about God. Don't let dire circumstances cause you to dishonor your relationship with God.

Jesus promised to send them the Holy Spirit to help them stay strong in His absence. He told them He couldn't send them the Holy Spirit unless He went away. Jesus explained to His disciples that it would be best for them if He left. The word *"best"* or *"expedient"* (KJV) found in John 16:7 is *sumphero*, a New Testament word that means "profitable."[14] Jesus left them because He loved them. Christ wanted the best for His disciples. He knew that the Holy Spirit would come to live in them, so God would constantly be with His followers. The most profitable life is filled with the Holy Spirit of God.

Jesus used the word *paraklétos* to describe the Holy Spirit. It is a compound Greek word consisting of *pará*, "from close beside," and *kaleó*, "to call." Thus, the Holy Spirit is called to come beside those who follow Jesus Christ. The English translations use the following words in John 16:7: "helper," "comforter," and "advocate."[15]

---

13. "4624. Skandalizó," BibleHub, accessed March 6, 2025, https://biblehub.com/greek/4624.htm.
14. "4851. Sumphero," BibleHub, accessed March 6, 2025, https://biblehub.com/greek/4851.htm.
15. "3875. Paraklétos," BibleHub, accessed March 6, 2025, https://biblehub.com/greek/3875.htm.

We have an advocate in the Holy Spirit who fights for and with us. The Holy Spirit encourages you in this life filled with difficult situations. God knew we needed help, so He sent us the Helper. God always gives us exactly what we need to live the life He has purposed for us.

Application:

How much do you rely on the Holy Spirit to encourage you? What are your thoughts on Jesus saying it was best that He left so that He could send the Holy Spirit?

Prayer:

Thank You for always giving me exactly what I need to follow You. Holy Spirit, immerse me in Your presence so I can confront life with the bravery and assurance You grant....

Day 49

SCRIPTURE READING: JOHN 16:16–33

Key Verses: John 16:16–22

> "In a little while you won't see me anymore. But a little while after that, you will see me again."
>
> Some of the disciples asked each other, "What does he mean when he says, 'In a little while you won't see me, but then you will see me,' and 'I am going to the Father'? And what does he mean by 'a little while'? We don't understand."
>
> Jesus realized they wanted to ask him about it, so he said, "Are you asking yourselves what I meant? I said in a little while you won't see me, but a little while after that you will see me again. I tell you the truth, you will weep and mourn over what is going to happen to me, but the world will rejoice. You will grieve, but your grief will suddenly turn to wonderful joy. It will be like a woman suffering the pains of labor. When her child is born, her anguish gives way to joy because she has brought a new baby into the world. So you have sorrow now, but I will see you again; then you will rejoice, and no one can rob you of that joy."

Explanation:

Jesus knew what His followers didn't: He would die a cruel death, but three days later, He would rise again! When He died, His disciples would face incredible grief. They would weep and mourn over His death while the world would rejoice that Jesus had died. However, Jesus gave them this fantastic encouragement: Their grief would suddenly become incredible joy!

The resurrection of Jesus Christ would change everything for His first followers—and it has changed everything for every follower since! Jesus can turn death to life, darkness to light, despair to joy, and the stain of sin into forgiveness that is white as snow.

Jesus knew that for His disciples, the celebration of victory over death would overcome the pain of their loss. Jesus compares their future joy to a mother giving birth to her child. (See John 16:21.) When a woman gives birth, she has sorrow because of her pain. However, when her baby is born, her joy at the gift of a child replaces the memory of her pain.

What Jesus accomplished on the cross and at the empty tomb brings victory over sin, death, the grave, and hell. The joy of Jesus has the power to overcome grief. A relationship with Christ brings new experiences and powerful moments that transform our lives and give us new and joy-filled memories.

If that is not enough good news, Jesus adds this statement in John 16:22: *"So you have sorrow now, but I will see you again; then you will rejoice, and no one can rob you of that joy."* The joy Jesus brings through the power of His resurrection is a joy that can never be taken away.

When you find true satisfaction in a walk with Jesus, the world cannot steal your joy. Since Jesus lives and reigns eternally, He will forever be our unshakeable source of joy.

Application:

How can patience and your willingness to trust God assure you that God can turn your grief into joy?

Prayer:

Jesus, You are so powerful that You provide resurrection power and joy over sadness. Thank You for preparing me for the tough times and filling my life with Your joy.…

Day 50

SCRIPTURE READING: JOHN 17:1–19

Key Verses: John 17:1–5

> *After saying all these things, Jesus looked up to heaven and said, "Father, the hour has come. Glorify your Son so he can give glory back to you. For you have given him authority over everyone. He gives eternal life to each one you have given him. And this is the way to have eternal life—to know you, the only true God, and Jesus Christ, the one you sent to earth. I brought glory to you here on earth by completing the work you gave me to do. Now, Father, bring me into the glory we shared before the world began."*

Explanation:

Jesus knew that the hour had come for the reason He came. It was time for Him to face the painful death on the cross and carry the burden of the world's sins. It was the designated time for the Lord to become the Lamb. (See John 1:29.)

What did Jesus do first when it was time for Him to face His most difficult situation? He prayed! If the Son of God sought the Father in prayer, how much more should we call out to God in prayer?

Jesus set His face toward His Father because He strongly desired to bring glory to God. Jesus knew that if God glorified His Son, then He could give the glory back to God.

What does it mean for us to glorify God? In John 17:1 the New Testament verb *doxazó*, is defined as, "to glorify, to honor, or to praise. It describes giving honor and praise to God."[16] You may have grown up in church and remember singing the doxology that began with, "Praise God from whom all blessings flow; Praise Him all creatures here below…" "Doxology" comes from the word *doxa* and *logos*, which means "word or speech." So, the doxology is "the glory speech" or "the word of praise ascribed to God." Therefore, Jesus was devoted to His prayer life and desire to bring praise and glory to God.

Jesus shares a profound insight into salvation during His prayer to the Father. Jesus prayed, *"And this is the way to have eternal life—to know you, the only true God, and Jesus Christ, the one you sent to earth"* (John 17:3). We do not inherit eternal life with Jesus because we know about Him. Our salvation comes through knowing Jesus and experiencing a personal relationship with Him. The word *"know"* in verse 3 is the Greek word *ginóskó*.[17] This word means to know somebody intimately. This word doesn't describe perfect knowledge but progressive knowledge that takes place over time through a consistent effort. It is the same word used to describe the union between a husband and a wife. Those who know Jesus personally belong to His church, the bride

---
16. "1392. Doxazó," BibleHub, accessed March 6, 2025, https://biblehub.com/greek/1392.htm.
17. "1097. Ginóskó," BibleHub, accessed March 6, 2025, https://biblehub.com/greek/1097.htm.

of Christ. As we continue in our relationship with God, we grow to know Him better and love Him more.

Jesus continues in His prayer by telling the Father that He completed the work the Father had given Him to do. Jesus's death on the cross and His resurrection from the grave have provided everything we need for salvation. All that is left for us to do is believe in Him by knowing Him personally. We can also bring glory to God by following His will and finishing whatever work He has called us to.

Application:

In what ways do Jesus's prayer life and His desire to glorify God encourage and teach you in your walk with Him?

Prayer:

Jesus, thank You for being a perfect example of a strong prayer life with the Father with a genuine desire to bring glory to God. God, may I know Your Son Jesus personally and bring glory to You....

Day 51

SCRIPTURE READING: JOHN 17:20–26

Key Verses: John 17:20–26

I am praying not only for these disciples but also for all who will ever believe in me through their message. I pray that they will all be one, just as you and I are one—as you are in me, Father, and I am in you. And may they be in us so that the world will believe you sent me.

I have given them the glory you gave me, so they may be one as we are one. I am in them and you are in me. May they experience such perfect unity that the world will know that you sent me and that you love them as much as you love me. Father, I want these whom you have given me to be with me where I am. Then they can see all the glory you gave me because you loved me even before the world began!

O righteous Father, the world doesn't know you, but I do; and these disciples know you sent me. I have revealed you to them, and I will continue to do so. Then your love for me will be in them, and I will be in them.

Explanation:

We have the privilege of reading Jesus's prayer to the Father in John 17. His prayer can be divided into three sections. First, He prayed for Himself (see verses 1–5). Second, He prayed for His disciples (see verses 6–19). Third, He prayed for every believer who would ever follow God (see verses 20–26).

In the final section of Jesus's prayer, you and I are on His heart. Jesus is praying for us to have unity like He and the Father possess. Jesus discloses this vital truth in verses 21 and 23: The unity of the believers will prove to the world that God sent His Son.

R. Kent Hughes explains the unity Jesus prayed for:

Christ prays for a supernatural unity that is modeled and enabled by the Godhead. This unity is possible because true believers are united in the core of their beings. That is why we often can sense that we have met another believer before words have even been spoken. We share the divine nature!

The closer we draw to Christ, the closer we draw to one another. Our unity can be described as an inverted cone, with God at the top and believers around the base. As we ascend the slopes of the cone, drawing nearer to God, we draw closer to our fellow believers. At the pinnacle (in God) we touch one another in deepest joy.[18]

Never underestimate the power of the unity of the believers. Don't ever doubt that Jesus loves you and is praying

---

18. R. Kent Hughes, *John: That You May Believe: Preaching the Word* (Crossway Books, 1999), 407–8.

to the Father on your behalf. Not only did He pray for us in John 17, but He is continually interceding for us now at the right hand of God. (See Romans 8:34.) In Hebrews 7:25, we learn that Jesus lives forever to intercede with God on our behalf!

Let those words sink into your heart today: Jesus is praying for you! You have the incredible privilege of praying to God, and Jesus lives to pray for you. Jesus truly does love you, and He greatly desires that you live within God's will for your life.

Jesus concludes His prayer with some further profound revelation to His children. God's love for Jesus will be in us, and Jesus will be with us. (See John 17:26.) The love that God has for His Son resides inside His followers, while Jesus walks with us constantly.

Application:

Can you imagine anything better than God loving you and never leaving you? What are your thoughts on Jesus praying for you?

Prayer:

Jesus, thank You for praying for me. Please remind me daily that God's love is in me, and You are with me....

Day 52

SCRIPTURE READING: JOHN 18:1–14

Key Verses: John 18:1–8

> After saying these things, Jesus crossed the Kidron Valley with his disciples and entered a grove of olive trees. Judas, the betrayer, knew this place, because Jesus had often gone there with his disciples. The leading priests and Pharisees had given Judas a contingent of Roman soldiers and Temple guards to accompany him. Now with blazing torches, lanterns, and weapons, they arrived at the olive grove.
>
> Jesus fully realized all that was going to happen to him, so he stepped forward to meet them. "Who are you looking for?" he asked.
>
> "Jesus the Nazarene," they replied.
>
> "I AM he," Jesus said. (Judas, who betrayed him, was standing with them.) As Jesus said "I AM he," they all drew back and fell to the ground! Once more he asked them, "Who are you looking for?"
>
> And again they replied, "Jesus the Nazarene."
>
> "I told you that I AM he," Jesus said. "And since I am the one you want, let these others go."

Explanation:

Notice the strange conglomerate of people who arranged for Jesus's arrest. First, those who set up the arrest were leading priests and Pharisees. Then, those who went to arrest Jesus consisted of His betrayer Judas, with a contingent of Roman soldiers and temple guards. Therefore, a former follower of Jesus is mixed up with Roman soldiers who are conversing with a Jewish priest. The only time these people ever got together was so they could execute Jesus Christ, who was sent to be the Savior of the world.

Scripture tells us that Jesus fully knew what would happen to Him. (See John 18:4.) Jesus knew that His death was imminent. He also knew the type of execution that He would surrender to. Yet, with complete composure and resolve, He submitted to His Father's will.

In this encounter, Jesus asked them who they were looking for twice. He knew they were looking for Him, so why ask the question even once? Furthermore, why ask it twice? I believe Jesus asked the question twice so that He could proclaim to them exactly who He is.

Both times (verses 5 and 8), Jesus answers with the exact two Greek words: *Egó eimi*, translated as "I am." *Egó eimi* is the identical structure used by John's Gospel in the seven "I AM" statements of Christ. You can't see it in English, but "I" is written twice in Greek. Greek scholars refer to it as the *egó eimi* construction. *Egó* is the pronoun "I." *Eimi* is the main verb of this verse. This verb is in the following tense—present active indicative, first person singular. By itself, the verb translates as "I am." The *egó eimi* construction means, "I, I am." Most Greek scholars define it as "I even I." So Jesus asked a question twice that He already knew the answer to so that He could emphatically tell them He is the great "I AM." His answer was so powerful that His reply threw them all to the ground!

Application:

Do you recognize that Jesus is the great "I AM ?" Who He is has the power to change who you are. How does Jesus's "I even I" response convey His desire for a personal and powerful relationship with you?

Prayer:

Thank You for sharing who You are so I can know You by name. Help me to trust that You are the "I AM" that has the power to meet any and every need in my life....

Day 53

SCRIPTURE READING: JOHN 18:15–27

Key Verses: John 18:15–18, 25–27

> Simon Peter followed Jesus, as did another of the disciples. That other disciple was acquainted with the high priest, so he was allowed to enter the high priest's courtyard with Jesus. Peter had to stay outside the gate. Then the disciple who knew the high priest spoke to the woman watching at the gate, and she let Peter in. The woman asked Peter, "You're not one of that man's disciples, are you?"
>
> "No," he said, "I am not."
>
> Because it was cold, the household servants and the guards had made a charcoal fire. They stood around it, warming themselves, and Peter stood with them, warming himself....
>
> Meanwhile, as Simon Peter was standing by the fire warming himself, they asked him again, "You're not one of his disciples, are you?"
>
> He denied it, saying, "No, I am not."
>
> But one of the household slaves of the high priest, a relative of the man whose ear Peter had cut off, asked, "Didn't I see you out there in the olive grove with

Jesus?" Again Peter denied it. And immediately a rooster crowed.

Explanation:

Have you ever blown it? Have you really messed up at some point in your past? I have on several occasions. Spiritually, I have been right where Peter is in John 18. If we are all honest, we all have found ourselves at a place we never thought we'd be.

This is how Peter's downward spiral began. His pride caused him to underestimate his capability to sin. Matthew's Gospel tells us that Peter had told Jesus earlier that he would never deny Him. (See Matthew 26:35.) Peter was so emphatic about even the thought of denying Jesus that he added these words: *"Even if I have to die with you, I will never deny you"* (Matthew 26:35).

I've said the same thing. I imagine you have, too. When we witnessed somebody else fail in an area where we never thought we could or would, we thought: "God, I would never _____." (Fill in the blank with your situation.)

It might be painful, but let's remember for a moment the pain of our sin. Hopefully, you have confessed it and found God's forgiveness. While God chooses to forget your sin, sometimes remembering the pain it caused can motivate you never to repeat that mistake. In my case, I asked God never to take away the memory of my pain because I don't ever want to experience that pain again in my life. My monumental mistakes and blatant sins hurt many people, especially those I love the most.

First and foremost, my sin was against God. Psalm 51:4 records David's words after his sin: *"Against you, and you only, have I sinned; I have done what is evil in your sight."* While David knew his sin hurt others, he first saw it as an outright defiance of God.

Peter denied Jesus not once or even twice but three times. God gave Peter three chances to get it right, but he still failed every time. If it can happen to Peter, it can happen to anyone. Even if we never denied Him with our lips, we could deny Him by how we live our lives.

Application:

We know God forgives, and He will restore Peter. Yet, why is sin so costly, and how can you remain faithful to God?

Prayer:

God, please remind me that I am only one decision away from denying You through my actions. May my lips always confess Your name and my life show how much I love You....

Day 54

SCRIPTURE READING: JOHN 18:28–40

Key Verses: John 18:33–37

> *Then Pilate went back into his headquarters and called for Jesus to be brought to him. "Are you the king of the Jews?" he asked him.*
>
> *Jesus replied, "Is this your own question, or did others tell you about me?"*
>
> *"Am I a Jew?" Pilate retorted. "Your own people and their leading priests brought you to me for trial. Why? What have you done?"*
>
> *Jesus answered, "My Kingdom is not an earthly kingdom. If it were, my followers would fight to keep me from being handed over to the Jewish leaders. But my Kingdom is not of this world."*
>
> *Pilate said, "So you are a king?"*
>
> *Jesus responded, "You say I am a king. Actually, I was born and came into the world to testify to the truth. All who love the truth recognize that what I say is true."*

Explanation:

After Jesus was arrested, He went through six different trials. Three trials were religious (Jewish), and three were civil (Roman). Here is a brief synopsis of the six trials.

Religious Trials
1. Annas (John 18:12–14)
2. Caiaphas (Matthew 26:57–68)
3. Sanhedrin (Luke 22:66–71)

Civil Trials
1. Pilate (John 18:28–38)
2. Herod (Luke 23:6–12)
3. Pilate again (John 18:39–19:6)

The religious trials falsely concluded that Jesus was a sinner. The civil trials decided that Jesus was innocent but sentenced Him to death regardless. So oddly enough, it was the religious leaders who found fault with Jesus, while the Roman authorities could find nothing wrong with Him! Yet Roman officials handed Jesus over for crucifixion because they caved to the peer pressure of popular opinion.

In today's Scripture, we find ourselves in Jesus's civil trial under Pontius Pilate. Pilate questioned Jesus about being the King of the Jews. In doing so, Jesus clearly stated that He was indeed a King, but His Kingdom was not of this Earth.

Truth is a major characteristic of the heavenly kingdom, of which Jesus is the King. On Earth, many people try to rule through lies. Even the religious leaders of Jesus's day told lies about Him. They even drummed up false witnesses and false charges against Christ. (See Matthew 26:59–63.)

Amid lies, Jesus said very little in His defense. Jesus did not spend too much time arguing against their lies because He was submitting to His Father's plan to offer forgiveness to sinners. The reality is that this life is not all there is. Our existence here is temporary; this world is not our everlasting home. One day, we will breathe our last breath and transition to our eternal destination. If we trust the truth of who Jesus is, we will live forever in His everlasting kingdom, where Jesus reigns as King. One day, we will finally experience the truth of who He is and will be forever set free.

Application:

What does it mean to you that Jesus is King of a kingdom that is not of this world? What does it mean for you that Jesus always testifies to the truth?

Prayer:

Lord, help me prepare for my eternal home where You rule and reign as King. Please guide me in understanding the truth of what You testify....

Day 55

SCRIPTURE READING: JOHN 19:1–22

Key Verses: John 19:13–20

> When they said this, Pilate brought Jesus out to them again. Pilate sat down on the judgment seat on the platform that is called the Stone Pavement (in Hebrew, Gabbatha). It was now about noon on the day of preparation for the Passover. And Pilate said to the people, "Look, here is your king!"
>
> "Away with him," they yelled. "Away with him! Crucify him!"
>
> "What? Crucify your king?" Pilate asked.
>
> "We have no king but Caesar," the leading priests shouted back.
>
> Then Pilate turned Jesus over to them to be crucified. So they took Jesus away. Carrying the cross by himself, he went to the place called Place of the Skull (in Hebrew, Golgotha). There they nailed him to the cross. Two others were crucified with him, one on either side, with Jesus between them. And Pilate posted a sign on the cross that read, "Jesus of Nazareth, the King of the Jews." The place where Jesus was crucified was near the

> city, and the sign was written in Hebrew, Latin, and
> Greek, so that many people could read it.

Explanation:

John explains Jesus's second trial before Pilate with several key details. First, notice the place where Pilate brings Jesus out for this final verdict. Pilate sat down on the judgment seat on a platform called the Stone Pavement. (See John 19:13.) *Exploring the Gospel of John* by John Phillips provides excellent insight into this place.

> Accordingly he [Pilate] seated himself on the judgment seat (*bema*). This was a raised platform with a seat in the open court in front of the praetorium. It was called "the pavement" (*lithostrotos*); the word literally means "strewn with stone" and suggests some kind of mosaic. In the vernacular of the Jews, in Hebrew (Aramaic), it was called *Gabbatha* ("the ridge").
>
> John gives this detail because of the solemnity of both place and occasion. He who is one day to sit on His own *bema* (Romans 14:10; 2 Corinthians 5:10) and who one day is to judge all the wicked dead (Revelation 20:11–15) was about to have sentence passed on Him by Jew and gentile alike.[19]

John also gives us the timing of these events. This occurred around noon on the day of preparation for the Passover. (See John 19:14.) This is the exact time lambs would be slaughtered to observe the Passover. This perfect timing points back to when John the Baptist proclaimed

---

19. John Phillips, *Exploring the Gospel of John: An Expository Commentary*. The John Phillips Commentary Series (Kregel Publications, 2001), 361.

concerning Jesus: *"Look! The Lamb of God who takes away the sin of the world!"* (John 1:29). Jesus came to Earth to fulfill one purpose: to offer Himself as the final sacrificial Lamb as a substitute offering to cover our sins.

When Pilate made his final verdict, and while lambs were being slaughtered outside Jerusalem, God was allowing His Son, who knew no sin, to become the offering for our sin so that we could be made right with God through Jesus Christ. (See 2 Corinthians 5:21.) While wayward people judged God's Son, God placed the judgment for our sins on His only Son.

Application:

Do you fully comprehend all that Jesus did for you at the cross? Spend some time today thinking about how much God loves you.

Prayer:

Jesus, You paid the ultimate sacrifice for my forgiveness. In doing so, You experienced God's judgment for all my sins. These words are not enough, but they are a start: Thank You! I love You. I need You....

Day 56

SCRIPTURE READING: JOHN 19:23–42

Key Verses: John 19:23–30

When the soldiers had crucified Jesus, they divided his clothes among the four of them. They also took his robe, but it was seamless, woven in one piece from top to bottom. So they said, "Rather than tearing it apart, let's throw dice for it." This fulfilled the Scripture that says, "They divided my garments among themselves and threw dice for my clothing." So that is what they did.

Standing near the cross were Jesus' mother, and his mother's sister, Mary (the wife of Clopas), and Mary Magdalene. When Jesus saw his mother standing there beside the disciple he loved, he said to her, "Dear woman, here is your son." And he said to this disciple, "Here is your mother." And from then on this disciple took her into his home.

Jesus knew that his mission was now finished, and to fulfill Scripture he said, "I am thirsty." A jar of sour wine was sitting there, so they soaked a sponge in it, put it on a hyssop branch, and held it up to his lips. When Jesus had tasted it, he said, "It is finished!" Then he bowed his head and gave up his spirit.

Explanation:

Today, we come to the cross of Christ at Calvary. As we look at Jesus's sacrificial death on the cross, may the following Scriptures give us a fuller perception of His death:

But God showed his great love for us by sending Christ to die for us while we were still sinners. (Romans 5:8)

He gave His life to purchase freedom for everyone.
(1 Timothy 2:6)

*All of us, like sheep, have strayed away. We have left God's paths to follow our own. Yet the L*ORD *laid on Him the sins of us all.* (Isaiah 53:6)

As Jesus hung on the cross before a mob of people, His love was displayed for all humanity. In Jesus's first recorded words from the cross, He asked God to forgive those responsible for His death. (See Luke 23:34.)

In John 19:26, Jesus displays great love and respect for His earthly mother. In today's terminology, His words may not sound respectful. If anyone of us called our mother "woman," that might not end too well. However, the word Jesus uses in the language of the New Testament was used in biblical times to show honor and profound love. Jesus loved Mary so much that He wanted to ensure she was provided for and protected after His departure.

The last words recorded by John of Jesus on the cross were, *"It is finished"* (John 19:30). These words portray the finality of His finished work for our salvation. Jesus's death on the cross entirely covered the sin debt we owed. Everything has been completed and fulfilled so that God can forgive our sins. Jesus's last breath on the cross would offer whoever would trust in Him their first opportunity to be fully forgiven. What Jesus finished provides a new start for all of us!

Application:

What do Jesus's words from the cross mean to you?

Prayer:

Jesus, Your words and sacrifice at the cross completed God's salvation plan. Your love was fully displayed that day at Calvary, and I will forever be grateful....

Day 57

SCRIPTURE READING: JOHN 20:1–18

Key Verses: John 20:1–8

> *Early on Sunday morning, while it was still dark, Mary Magdalene came to the tomb and found that the stone had been rolled away from the entrance. She ran and found Simon Peter and the other disciple, the one whom Jesus loved....*
>
> *Peter and the other disciple started out for the tomb. They were both running, but the other disciple outran Peter and reached the tomb first. He stooped and looked in and saw the linen wrappings lying there, but he didn't go in. Then Simon Peter arrived and went inside. He also noticed the linen wrappings lying there, while the cloth that had covered Jesus' head was folded up and lying apart from the other wrappings. Then the disciple who had reached the tomb first also went in, and he saw and believed.*

Explanation:

All red-blooded men around the world are passionate about competition. If you don't believe it, challenge any man to a friendly game of cornhole, basketball, or any athletic contest—and watch the unfriendliness of a contest emerge.

You can stay inside and see the same results if you challenge a man to a game of cards or even Monopoly! I believe God hard-wired men to compete.

Today's Scripture reveals the healthy competitive nature between two of Jesus's disciples, Peter and John. To fully perceive the depths of this, understand two truths. First, *"the other disciple"* is John's way of speaking of himself as he writes the Gospel of John. Second, God expresses Himself through the unique personality of the human author He created, guiding them as they write under the inspiration of the Holy Spirit.

Now reread John 20:3–8 and insert "I" in the place of *"the other disciple."* Doing so will give you a better understanding of John's account. It reads something like this:

> *Peter and [I] started out for the tomb. We were both running, but [I] outran Peter and reached the tomb first. [I] stooped and looked in and saw the linen wrappings lying there, but [I] didn't go in. Then Simon Peter arrived and went inside. He also noticed the linen wrappings lying there, while the cloth that had covered Jesus' head was folded up and lying apart from the other wrappings. Then [I] also went in, and [I] saw and believed.*

Healthy and humorous competition. Twice, John writes in God's eternal Word that he outran Peter. Then he implies that he respectfully didn't go in when he arrived first, but that slow but impulsive Peter just went right in. John finishes the account by saying that he only went in after Peter had walked in, and it was he who truly believed.

The competition between Peter and John is evident. John even wrote his Gospel using the designation *"the one Jesus loved."* You wouldn't like this terminology if you were one of Jesus's other disciples. Knowing I am much like Jesus's first disciples is encouraging. Sometimes, my competitive nature gets the best of me. I should use that same drive to succeed in following Jesus more closely.

Application:

Since we are so competitive about things that don't matter in the scheme of eternity, shouldn't we at least have a battling desire to follow Jesus and believe in His resurrection power?

Prayer:

Thank You for being patient with me when my priorities get out of order. Please give me a greater desire to win when it comes to following You....

Day 58

SCRIPTURE READING: JOHN 20:19–31

Key Verses: John 20:19–27

> That Sunday evening the disciples were meeting behind locked doors because they were afraid of the Jewish leaders. Suddenly, Jesus was standing there among them! "Peace be with you," he said. As he spoke, he showed them the wounds in his hands and his side. They were filled with joy when they saw the Lord! Again he said, "Peace be with you. As the Father has sent me, so I am sending you." Then he breathed on them and said, "Receive the Holy Spirit. If you forgive anyone's sins, they are forgiven. If you do not forgive them, they are not forgiven."
>
> One of the twelve disciples, Thomas (nicknamed the Twin), was not with the others when Jesus came. They told him, "We have seen the Lord!"
>
> But he replied, "I won't believe it unless I see the nail wounds in his hands, put my fingers into them, and place my hand into the wound in his side."
>
> Eight days later the disciples were together again, and this time Thomas was with them. The doors were locked; but suddenly, as before, Jesus was standing among them. "Peace be with you," he said. Then he

said to Thomas, "Put your finger here, and look at my hands. Put your hand into the wound in my side. Don't be faithless any longer. Believe!"

Explanation:

Thomas was known to be such a skeptic that later in church history, someone called him "Doubting Thomas." However, before criticizing Thomas for doubting the resurrection, put yourself in his sandals and consider what he was facing. Jesus had just been crucified three days earlier, and fear for His followers was at an all-time high. Who knew what the Roman and religious leaders would do now to those who were known associates of Jesus? To make matters worse for Thomas, many of his close friends had claimed to see the resurrected Jesus, but he hadn't seen Christ yet with his own eyes. Imagine all the questions running through Thomas's mind: "Why haven't I seen Jesus for myself? Could Christ be alive?" Doubt and faith must have fought mightily to control Thomas's mind while questions consumed his emotions.

Note that before Thomas received the nickname of "Doubting Thomas," Scripture tells us he already had a nickname: *"The Twin"* (John 20:24). Was it possible that Thomas had a twin brother or sister? If he did, the Bible never mentions his twin sibling by name.

We could be given his biblical nickname to examine our struggles with faith and doubt more closely. Could it be that, spiritually speaking, Thomas is your twin? Perhaps you struggle with doubt when others say Jesus performed a miracle in their lives. Do you have to see it to believe it regarding your faith journey?

How do you grow more in your faith so that your doubts will decrease? Jesus answered when He appeared to Thomas and showed him His scars. Christ said, *"Don't be faithless any longer. Believe!"* (John 20:27). Trusting Jesus daily will help your doubts fade. As you focus more on who Christ is and spiritually look at the sacrifice He made for your sins, God can move your perception from "seeing is believing" to "believing is seeing."

Application:
In what ways are you spiritually Thomas's twin?

Prayer:
God, forgive me for doubting You. I trust that You are more than able to help me overcome my doubts. Grow my faith more in You each day....

Day 59

SCRIPTURE READING: JOHN 21:1–14

Key Verses: John 21:3–9

Simon Peter said, "I'm going fishing."

"We'll come, too," they all said. So they went out in the boat, but they caught nothing all night.

At dawn Jesus was standing on the beach, but the disciples couldn't see who he was. He called out, "Fellows, have you caught any fish?"

"No," they replied.

Then he said, "Throw out your net on the right-hand side of the boat, and you'll get some!" So they did, and they couldn't haul in the net because there were so many fish in it.

Then the disciple Jesus loved said to Peter, "It's the Lord!"

When Simon Peter heard that it was the Lord, he put on his tunic (for he had stripped for work), jumped into the water, and headed to shore. The others stayed with the boat and pulled the loaded net to the shore, for they were only about a hundred yards from shore. When they got there, they found breakfast waiting for them—fish cooking over a charcoal fire, and some bread.

Explanation:

If you had gone looking for Simon Peter after Jesus's death, you would have found a sign on his door that said, "Gone Fishing!" Remember, Jesus had initially called Peter out of a life of fishing. (See Matthew 4:18–22.) Peter had denied Jesus three times. He was struggling with the guilt of failure and the fear of the unknown. So what did Peter do next? He went back to fishing.

What do people do when they don't know what to do? Many of them go back to their old way of life, back to the only thing they knew before they met Jesus. When you hit a roadblock in your faith journey and are overwhelmed and confused, you are tempted to fall back into your old nature. Some people go back to the bottle. Others revert to pain pills. Some withdraw into their world of pain and block out anyone who tries to help.

When we revert to our old ways, Jesus will rescue us and draw us back to Himself. Peter and a few other disciples are fishing and haven't caught anything. Jesus shows up at the shore, but they don't recognize Him. He tells them to cast on the right side of the boat, and they catch so many fish they can't pull their nets in. Peter recognizes Jesus, and they fellowship on the shore with a meal Jesus has prepared.

What is the moral of this story? It is always better to stay with Jesus! Jesus is the creator and sustainer of life, so it makes sense that your life goes much better when you follow Him. Jesus wants to change our lives and transform our nature. He wants to make all things new. For that to happen, we must leave behind our old way of living and follow Him into the newness of life.

Additionally, I love that Scripture tells us exactly how many fish they caught: 153 big fish. (See John 21:11.) They didn't even count the little ones, just the big ones. Sounds like fishermen to me! If you want a life that counts, go with Jesus. Just like the disciples, He can transform you into fishers of men. (See Matthew 4:19.)

Application:

In what ways are you tempted to fall back into your old ways? How can you stay close to Jesus so He can continue to transform your life?

Prayer:

I praise You for rescuing me from my old nature. Help me to follow You consistently, as You make me more like You....

Day 60

SCRIPTURE READING: JOHN 21:15–25

Key Verses: John 21:17–22

> A third time he asked him, "Simon son of John, do you love me?"
>
> Peter was hurt that Jesus asked the question a third time. He said, "Lord, you know everything. You know that I love you."
>
> Jesus said, "Then feed my sheep.
>
> "I tell you the truth, when you were young, you were able to do as you liked; you dressed yourself and went wherever you wanted to go. But when you are old, you will stretch out your hands, and others will dress you and take you where you don't want to go." Jesus said this to let him know by what kind of death he would glorify God. Then Jesus told him, "Follow me."
>
> Peter turned around and saw behind them the disciple Jesus loved—the one who had leaned over to Jesus during supper and asked, "Lord, who will betray you?" Peter asked Jesus, "What about him, Lord?"
>
> Jesus replied, "If I want him to remain alive until I return, what is that to you? As for you, follow me."

Explanation:

Peter had denied Jesus three times. (See John 18:15–27.) In these closing verses of John's Gospel, we see Jesus fully restoring Peter. Jesus asks Peter three times, *"Do you love Me?"* Three questions, one for each denial. After the third question, Scripture tells us that Peter was hurt. (See John 21:17.)

Questions have a way of opening old wounds while at the same time bringing healing. If you don't deal with the pain and mistakes of your past, you can never find complete healing and full restoration. So Jesus repeatedly questions Peter about His love for Him so that Peter will think deeply about their relationship. Thank goodness we serve a God who seeks to forgive our past sins and restore us to a right relationship with Him.

This is a monumental moment in Peter's spiritual journey with Jesus. Jesus forgives and restores Peter, concluding with a final calling: *"Follow Me."* At this point in Scripture, you would think the following words out of Peter's mouth would be: "Yes, Sir! Thank You, Jesus! I love You!" But instead, Peter turns around and sees John and asks Jesus, "What about him?"

Peter falls into the comparison trap in the most significant moment of his life thus far with Jesus. He takes his eyes off Jesus's high calling and worries about what somebody else is doing. In your journey with Jesus, don't get distracted by what others are doing or not doing for Jesus! God has a specific plan for your life. He created you to follow His calling for your life. The world doesn't require a duplicate of anyone; it needs your uniqueness.

Listen closely to Jesus's reply to Peter's comparison: *"What is that to you? As for you, follow me"* (John 21:22). Jesus redirects Peter back to his calling. Keep your focus on Jesus and follow Him into the future He has planned for you!

Application:

How do you keep your eyes off others to focus more on Jesus? As we conclude this study of John's Gospel, what have you learned about your relationship with Jesus? What do you need to apply to your life to follow Him faithfully?

Prayer:

Thank You, Jesus, for redirecting my focus back on You. Help me to surrender my life daily and dedicate my attention to You. A personal, growing relationship with You leads to a fulfilled and satisfied life....

CONCLUSION

Your thoughts will indeed determine your spiritual quality of life. The Proverb writer wrote, *"Guard your heart above all else, for it determines the course of your life"* (Proverbs 4:23). You are the gatekeeper for the thoughts that enter your mind. Each day, you choose which thoughts can enter and which are not permitted. Your continual thoughts then impact your words and actions. Your habitual thinking patterns will either encourage you toward spiritual maturity or keep you from becoming all that God desires you to be.

None of our thoughts are neutral. They are either focused on Jesus or the things of this world. Every thought that you meditate on in your mind moves you toward your God-given potential or away from it. The goal of *7 Minutes with Jesus for Men* was to start your day thinking about Jesus Christ by reading just a small portion of His Word and seeking to apply one additional truth from Scripture to your life. Hopefully, these seven minutes in God's Word have caused a chain reaction of godly thoughts that helped you focus on God's will throughout your day. May these last sixty days lead to a daily focus on Jesus that directs you to God's best for your life.

Prayer:

Thank You, Jesus, for these last sixty days of applying the gospel of John to my everyday life. May this journey through John create a disciplined pattern of starting each day with You. Help me to grow in my love for Your Word so that, in turn, it will cause me to grow more deeply in love with You....

ABOUT THE AUTHOR

Dr. Ray Cummings has pastored churches in Mississippi and Alabama for over eighteen years and has been in ministry for over thirty years. He resides in Purvis, Mississippi, and serves as senior pastor at Hattiesburg Community Church. He graduated from William Carey College in 1992 with a bachelor's degree in pre-med. He attended New Orleans Baptist Theological Seminary where he received a master of divinity with languages degree in 1996 and a doctor of ministry specializing in church growth and evangelism in 2001.

He has been married to his partner in ministry, Amanda Burge Cummings, since December 6, 1997. They have three sons: Carter, who is married to Hope; Camron; and Moses, along with one daughter named Mercy. They have a nonprofit named after their daughter called "Mercy's Mission" that feeds and educates children in the Lisa Center orphanage in Goma, Congo. Ray loves preaching, writing, hunting, and anything sports-related.